STRANGE

TOPICS *Book #1*

Enigmatic Biblical Phenomena with Possibility of Interpretation: Day One - Before The Flood

BOOK #1 *of The *Serie:*
"Strange & Controversial Topics
with <u>Possibility of Interpretation;</u>
In the Old Testament of The Bible"

By José E. Espinoza © 2025

José E. Espinoza

José E. Espinoza

Dedication

To a <u>Human Being Interested</u> in the Biblical Records of the Holy Scriptures, with the Desire and Purpose <u>to Know and Understand</u> the <u>Secrets of the Kingdom </u> of God Today.

- José E. Espinoza

This Book Belong to:

_____

José E. Espinoza

Blessings and Enlightenment

In Your Life & Purpose

\- **José E. Espinoza**

José E. Espinoza

Table of Contents

STRANGE TOPICS *Book #1*

José E. Espinoza

Introduction

Imagine opening a Bible and noticing that the stories of Genesis, familiar since childhood, bristle with riddles you've never really seen. Maybe you're a seeker, a student, or someone who has heard these tales countless times in church pews; yet, beneath the surface, early Genesis hides **enigmas**, symbols, and phrases that have perplexed, inspired, and divided scholars for generations. The more closely you read, the stranger—and more compelling—the text becomes.

This book is written for you—the adult or young adult reader ready to move beyond Sunday school versions and embrace the enigmas at the Bible's heart. It invites thoughtful Christians, students of theology, curious skeptics, religious educators, and anyone intrigued by the roots of spiritual tradition to journey through Genesis with new eyes. Here we dare to ask hard questions without fear, holding up each strange and controversial moment to the light of interpretation, history, and honest inquiry.

Genesis reveals humanity as a paradox. Made from dust, yet animated by breath of God; innocent, yet destined to fall; naked, yet unashamed—until knowledge awakens shame and the urge to hide. When Adam and Eve reach for the forbidden tree, whether that fruit was apple, fig, or something forever lost to history, they cross a threshold that alters every life thereafter. The story's ambiguity—its refusal to define the fruit—reminds us that some knowledge comes at a price, and that the real question is not simply "what" they ate, but "why."

Layer upon layer, these first stories invite us into debates that still stir today. Was the serpent a mere animal, or something more—a vessel for evil itself, or a mirror for human doubt? Why does God respond to disobedience with both judgment and mercy, making garments of skin for the newly aware couple, refusing to abandon them even as He bars the way back to Eden? The flaming sword and cherubim stand not just as punishment, but as paradoxical signs—barriers that also protect, reminders that restoration is possible but never cheap or simple.

Within seeming tangents—like the mysterious mark set upon Cain—we discover new questions about justice, punishment, and grace. When God marks the world's first murderer, is it retribution, protection, or a warning against cycles of vengeance? The brief mention of 3 women only like Adah, Zillah, and Naamah, while others remain nameless, compels us to consider whose stories get told, whose voices matter, and how memory itself is shaped by silence as much as speech.

And despite the bleakness of exile, broken trust, and wandering, Genesis quietly unveils a turning point. People, weary of violence and alienation, begin once more to "call on the name of the Lord." The act is more than ritual—it's a communal cry for restoration, hope, and relationship that had been shattered. In that moment, God's seemingly distant kingdom finds a foothold in wounded human hearts, sparking the long story of reconciliation that runs through all Scripture and reaches into the present day.

Why should any of this matter now, thousands of years after the rain stopped falling outside Noah's ark? Because these "strange topics" are not relics, but reflections—mirrors in which we see our own doubts, hopes, and longings. The mysteries of Genesis challenge us to think deeply, to hold our interpretations with humility, and to seek wisdom that transcends facile answers. They remind us that faith is not blind certainty but courageous engagement: a willingness to ask, to wrestle, and finally, to rest in the hands of a God who welcomes questioning souls.

As we embark on this journey together, you'll find no simplistic solutions here—no promises that every controversy will be settled or every riddle neatly solved. Instead, you are invited to bring your mind and heart fully into conversation with the text, to embrace complexity as a sign of sacred depth rather than confusion, and to discover that some of the Bible's most powerful teachings emerge precisely from what remains unresolved.

"Strange Topics Before the Flood" beckons the curious and the committed, the scholar and the searcher, to encounter Genesis anew—not as a tidy introduction to faith, but as a living, challenging testament to humanity's greatest questions. As you turn these pages, you'll gain interpretive tools, historical context, and fresh perspectives, along with encouragement to keep seeking, keep asking, and keep growing in the rich soil of **biblical mystery**.

Welcome to a conversation as old as civilization and as urgent as your next prayer. Welcome to the story behind the stories, where strangeness is not a problem, but an invitation—to wonder, to dig deeper, and to let ancient mysteries illuminate your own path of faith.

Part 1:

Prima EPOCH

(Primary Era of Strange & Enigmatic Phenomena)

Attention!

- Let us keep in mind the remark, that no matter who say it, or how eloquent anyone proclaim some commentaries, in reference to any portion of the <u>Sacred Scriptures,</u> without much literal details, (**unless it is written in the text with the correspondent explanation),** <u>in relation</u> to <u>any of the following topics,</u> 'in this book,' and 'throughout the rest of the bible,' In resume: **'it is honestly and humbly <u>a possibility of interpretation'</u>**. Nothing more, nothing less.

- José E. Espinoza

Chapter 1:

Strange 'DAY ONE'

When? How? How Long?

(A Day absent of Time)

(GENESIS 1:5)

"*...And there was evening and there was morning, <u>one day.</u>*"

A Day Before the Measure of Time

Genesis 1:1 begins with the profound statement, "In the beginning, God created the heavens and the earth." Then, **Genesis 1:5** conclude; ***"And there was evening and there was morning, <u>one day.</u>"*** This chapter explores the meaning of "day" in the creation narrative. Where it is mentioned as 'one day' or 'day one', before the <u>Solar System</u> establishment, as a function and principle to measure time. This '**<u>Day One</u>**' or 'One Day'; Was it a literal 24-hour period, an epoch spanning millennia, or a metaphor for divine acts beyond human comprehension? We will analyze some possibilities of interpretation, with the theological implications of each interpretation and its relevance to our understanding of God's creative power.

Mysterious/Controversial "<u>One Day</u>" or "<u>Day 1</u>" (Gen.1:5)

The concept of a "day" seems simple—twenty-four hours marked by sunrise and sunset—but what if the very first "day" described in **Genesis 1:5** existed before the sun or moon had been set in the sky? Without these familiar markers, how can we understand time itself at creation's dawn? Long before humans walked the earth, in a world without defined hours or celestial rhythms, the idea of counting days takes on a mysterious and almost poetic meaning. This challenges not only our sense of time but invites us to reconsider the nature of life as it was originally intended—pure, unbroken by weariness or decay, unfolding within a divinely ordered paradise. Here, the boundaries between divine purpose and human experience blur, revealing a reality where existence moves according to a rhythm far different from our own, shaped by harmony, caretaking, and presence rather than measurement and toil.

Interpreting the Mysterious 'One Day' or '<u>Day 1</u>' in Genesis 1:5

A world without the sun or moon, without living creatures to mark the passage of time, forms the mysterious backdrop for the phrase **"<u>One Day</u>" or "Day 1" (depending on the Biblical Version) in <u>Genesis 1:5</u>.** In the silence and darkness of the primordial Earth, God's voice calls out, *"Let there be light,"* (Genesis 1:3) and light pierces the void. This division of light from darkness, described as the **first "<u>day</u>,"** predates both organic life and the ordinary means by which humans later measure time—namely, the rhythm of the sun and moon established only (later) in **Genesis 1:14.** where God creates *<u>lights in the expanse</u> of the heavens to separate the day from the night."* Remarking this portion of the Scripture (Genesis 1:14 to Genesis 1:19.) *"A <u>Fourt Day</u>"*. **The meaning of "One Day"** here in **Genesis 1:5** is anything but straightforward and raises fundamental questions about how time itself is conceived in the very first chapters of biblical history.

José E. Espinoza

At this early point in the narrative, nothing we understand as living is present. No creatures witness the dawn, and no humans stand to count the hours. The usual signposts of time—a sunrise, a chime, a clock— are absent because no celestial bodies have yet been assigned the job of marking days and nights. The text's narrative instead simply divides the emergence of light and darkness into what it calls "day," offering no external reference point. As a result, how readers and theologians understand this "day" deeply affects every subsequent **interpretation** of the creation week.

Possibilities of Interpretation:

Two broad Primary interpretive traditions have developed to address this puzzle.

The <u>First</u> Possibility of Interpretation:

One tradition understands the "One Day" as an **epoch** or **era**, a span whose boundaries are shaped by divine action rather than human reckoning. Supporters of this view often highlight the poetic and symbolic qualities of the text. The Hebrew word for "<u>day</u>," **yohm,** appears throughout Scripture in contexts that clearly mean more than a strict 24-hour period. For instance, later in **Genesis chapter 2: verse 4**, a summary describes *"<u>the day that Jehovah God made earth and heaven,</u>"* referring not to one dawn-to-dusk event but to **the whole era of creation**. Scholarly works point out that, just as in Numbers 14:34 or Ezekiel 4:6, biblical language often uses "**<u>day</u>**" to <u>symbolize longer periods</u>, such as a year or a prophetic **age**.

José E. Espinoza

Additionally, **the absence of the sun** <u>until</u> **<u>the fourth creation day</u>** challenges the typical, literal approach to what constitutes a "**day**." <u>Without the sun</u>, 'the mechanism by which evening and morning could cycle' as we understand them is, at the least, '<u>obscure</u>'. Some interpreters suggest that the "evening and morning" structure serves a literary function, marking the **phases of creative activity** without anchoring them to astronomical events. This reading sees the Genesis narrative as accessible to ancient listeners, using familiar terms and images <u>to capture the grandeur of creation</u> rather than providing a technical account.

Second Possibility of Interpretation:

The other tradition insists on the literalness of the narrative's language. Here, "One Day" is a 24-hour interval. Proponents often root their understanding in the patterned repetition of "there was evening, and there was morning." This literal interpretation shapes key doctrines, reinforcing, for example, the framework for Sabbath rest and the pattern of human labor found in the Ten Commandments. It is argued that Genesis was written to be clear and understandable, not to cloak history in metaphor, and the six days of creation, directly ground the institution of work and rest cycles for Israel, consequently for the rest of Humanity.

Yet, even this approach faces significant questions. **Genesis 1:3 records the 'creation of light'** before the registered mention of the creation of the sun itself; (Genesis 1:14), and some critics ask whether this light could support a rigid sequence of terrestrial days. Others maintain that the omnipotence of God makes such mysteries irrelevant—if God declares "a day," it is, by definition, a day, and human science or logic cannot limit divine action.

Layered atop this debate is the challenge posed by the scriptural principle that God's sense of time is fundamentally different from humanity's. Both **Psalms 90:4** "*A thousand years in your sight are like a day that has just gone by*" and 2 **Peter 3:8** declare that ***"one day is like a thousand years, and a thousand years like one day"*** before God, highlighting a perspective where time itself bends and stretches beyond mortal comprehension. This motif urges humility and creative openness in interpretation. The experience of time without sun, moon, or living measurement invites readers to imagine a reality sovereignly ordered yet unmeasured, where a "day" simply marks transition from one creative phase to another.

Summary & Reflections of this Topic

Having explored the complex meanings behind the **"One Day" of Genesis 1:5**, we gain a deeper appreciation for the unique nature of time, existence, and divine harmony at creation's dawn. This understanding invites us to approach Scripture with both humility and curiosity, recognizing that the early chapters of Genesis communicate truths that transcend ordinary human measures and expectations. With this fresh insight, we (as a habitual readers and/or scholars alike) can journey forward to uncover; how the unfolding biblical narrative continues to reveal the **profound mysteries of these strange topics**. And let us do it with positive intention, to search and create a better relationship between Creator, creation, and humanity's intended place within it.

José E. Espinoza

Chapter 2:

Enigmatic '<u>PLURALITY in GOD</u>'

Controversial Celestial Phrase; (?)

(GENESIS 1:26)

Then God Said, "*Let <u>Us</u> Make* Man in <u>*Our*</u> *image*," According to <u>*Our*</u> *Likeness…*

Strange Divine Deliberation in the Plurality: '<u>Let Us Make</u> Man'

When reading the opening verses of Genesis, most people expect a straightforward account of creation led by a singular God. Yet, embedded in this familiar text is a puzzling phrase: ***<u>Let us</u> make man <u>in our</u> image.*** The shift from singular to plural language invites questions that have intrigued theologians, scholars, and believers for centuries. This unexpected use of "us" and "our" suggests a complex picture of divine identity and raises profound mysteries about how God relates to creation and to humanity.

This chapter delves into that rare and **remarkable <u>plural phrase,</u>** exploring the different ways it has been understood throughout history. We will examine ancient interpretations involving a divine council of heavenly beings and contrast these with Christian readings that see an early hint of the Trinity within God's nature. Along the way, we will consider how these perspectives shape ideas about human dignity, responsibility, and the special role people play as those made in the image of a God described not simply as one, but as more than one. Through careful reflection on scripture and theology, this chapter opens a window into one of the Bible's most fascinating and debated verses.

Rare Divine Council Debate; for <u>Possibilities</u> of <u>Interpretation</u>

A distinct shift appears in Genesis 1:26, where the singular Creator suddenly refers to **_"us"_** and **_"our"_** while declaring, *"Let us make man in our image, after our likeness."* This is more than a grammatical curiosity. Throughout Hebrew scripture, God typically speaks and acts in the singular—"And God said, 'Let there be light'…"—so the emergence of this plural marks a striking break from tradition. The wording seems to open a window into a moment of divine self-address or dialogue, <u>raising questions that echo through centuries</u> of theological pondering. Why the sudden plurality? Who is included in **this mysterious "us"**? These questions have catalyzed debates about the very nature and identity of God.

Possibility of Interpretation 1:

The **<u>Divine Council</u> interpretation** offers one path through this puzzle. Scholars who endorse this view draw on knowledge of ancient Near Eastern traditions, where gods are often depicted as presiding over celestial assemblies of divine beings. Biblical books such as Job and Psalms reference gatherings where divine entities appear before God—**Job 1:6** describes *"the sons of God"* presenting themselves before the Lord. Within this landscape, **Genesis 1:26** (for some interpreters) it is seen as God addressing an angelic or divine council. Supporters note that similar councils are present in Ugaritic and Mesopotamian literature, situating the Hebrew text within its broader, polytheistic cultural neighbors. This reading allows Genesis to reflect its ancient context, illustrating **God's role as supreme** <u>among a host of lesser spiritual beings</u> rather than in isolated solitude.

José E. Espinoza

The Divine Council perspective implies complex theological consequences. While it seeks historical and cultural integrity by aligning Genesis with its ancient environment, it generates controversy for potentially challenging the heart of Israel's monotheism. If God is depicted consulting with a council, does this threaten the uncompromising oneness that Deuteronomy insists upon? The challenge arises from verses like **Genesis 3:5**, in which the serpent says, ***"You will be like 'divine beings' [Elohim], *knowing good and evil,"*** and the term **"*knowers"** is plural, hinting at more than one entity. Traditional interpreters worry that expanding the scene to include a heavenly cabinet might blur the bright line between Creator and creature. Jewish and Christian commentators have long debated how to maintain God's singular supremacy while not ignoring the plural grammar woven into the narrative.

Possibility of Interpretation 2:

Alongside this view, Christian theologians have championed the **Trinitarian interpretation**, treating **Genesis 1:26** as a glimpse of the tri-personal nature of God. Here, <u>the Father addresses the Son and the Spirit</u>—a subtle but meaningful anticipation of later, explicit doctrines describing God as three Persons in one being. This reading is rooted not only in Christian tradition but buttressed by scriptural testimony: **John 1:3** claims, *"Through him all things were made,"* connecting creation directly to Christ. Job 33:4 and Psalm 104:30 extend creative agency to the Spirit. The New Testament authors echo this, linking humanity's creation "in our image" with being shaped to reflect Christ's likeness **(Romans 8:29; 1 John 3:2).**

author block
José E. Espinoza

Despite its theological elegance, the Trinitarian approach faces its own challenges. Critics argue that reading the Trinity into Genesis risks anachronism, importing later doctrinal developments into an ancient text that originally addressed an audience steeped in the strict monotheism of Israel. Hebrew never uses the so-called "plural of majesty" pronouns for monarchs elsewhere, so claiming that the plural is simply a royal we lack solid linguistic support in the Hebrew Bible. Later Christian creeds, though, used Genesis 1:26 as evidence that the seeds of the Trinitarian idea were present from the very beginning. This underscores a central tension: does the text intentionally plant a seed of multi-personed divinity, or are Christians finding echoes that the original authors never intended?

The impact of these plural pronouns reaches far beyond technical debate. Genesis 1:26 depicts a moment before humanity's existence—a pause for deliberation, as if God holds council, <u>whether with angelic hosts or within God's own triune being.</u> This moment offers a rare glimpse into divine intentionality and relationship. The decision, ***"Let us make man,"*** suggests that human identity bears traces of this complex unity—or community—at the heart of God. Whether one sees this as reflecting a heavenly court or the relational love within the Trinity, the formulation has shaped centuries of reflection on God's nature as involving a kind of fellowship rather than static solitude.

From this astonishing plural, questions flow naturally about the meaning of being made "in our image"—questions about unity, relationality, and the dignity invested in human beings. The divine deliberation suggests that humanity's role and destiny will be bound up with the mystery, depth, and responsibility of bearing a likeness to the God who is, in ways both singular and wonderfully plural.

José E. Espinoza

Ripple Effects: Human Uniqueness, Responsibility, and Theological Impact

The phrase "let us make man in our image" in Genesis 1:26 stands as one of the most discussed aspects of biblical language. This plural pronouncement draws countless readers into a deeper contemplation of God's nature and invites reflection on how human beings fit into the wider tapestry of creation. The use of "us" and "our" amplifies the special status of humanity, marking people as more than mere creatures among others. Instead, humans emerge as unique bearers of the 'imago Dei', a role that stretches across theological, philosophical, and ethical domains.

Exploring the meaning of this plural form, **theologians have posed divergent possibilities.** Some understand the language as signaling a council of divine beings, while others interpret it through the Christian doctrine of the Trinity, envisioning a conversation within the Godhead itself. No matter the path, both readings communicate a heightened importance for human identity. When viewed as a council of divine beings, the plural marks humanity as the product of divine deliberation, a creature designed by divine intention in the presence of others and with a purposeful place in the order of things. This can be contrasted with interpretations focusing on the Trinity, where the conversation occurs within God—implying a depth of communal life and engagement intrinsic to God's own being. In either case, the legacy left behind centers on human value. People gain dignity not just from their individual attributes, but from relationships they mirror or inhabit. The plural in Genesis subtly elevates humans above the rest of creation, endowing them with a likeness that is relational and dynamic, not merely functional or superficial.

Examining theological discourse, these interpretations inform doctrines about human dignity and ethical responsibility. Dignity, according to some traditional substance dualist readings, is rooted in the soul—an immaterial aspect that anchors personal identity and sets humans apart fundamentally.

Additional Possibility of Interpretation:

Other frameworks emphasize the **relational aspect** derived from the "let us make" phrase. In this view, humans are not islands but partners in a grand relational network reflecting the divine's own plurality. Specific examples in Christian theology include the New Testament themes of adoption into **God's family**, or Christ as the new Adam—each one emphasizing redeemed human nature, **collective destiny**, and a vocation tied directly to <u>God's deliberative will</u>. This shapes ethical traditions by suggesting that every person, by nature of being **<u>"in the image of God,"</u>** possesses inherent value, deserving care and respect regardless of <u>abilities or social status</u>.

Moving to the matter of **human agency and stewardship**, different readings of the plural language yield distinct consequences. A divine council perspective may empower humans as vice-regents, co-laborers sharing in God's stewardship. This cosmic partnership positions people **to exercise dominion over creation**, making choices that reflect the deliberate deliberation seen in the act of their own creation. Authority, in this context, is shared and participatory, grounding responsibility in shared dialogue with the divine. By contrast, the Trinitarian view accords humanity a personal, even intimate, relationship with God. Here, humans become echoes of divine community, whose agency is tested through trust, obedience, and loving engagement. The ethical requirements that spring from these views ripple into concrete dilemmas—in the divine council framework, ethical demands revolve around collective responsibility, whereas Trinitarian ethics may focus on authenticity, self-giving, and imitation of Christ as the perfect imago.

José E. Espinoza

Attention to destiny further sharpens the contrast between these outlooks. Some theologians frame human destiny as an open process that develops as people participate in the plurality of divine relationship. The very deliberation implied in "let us make" points to an ongoing, responsive journey—one where destiny is shaped by engagement and evolution within the divine-human partnership. Others argue for a closed design, where destiny is fixed by the will of a singular, sovereign God. These distinctions press into major theological debates: is humanity's fate open, shaped in the living encounter with God, or predetermined, unfolding precisely as decreed? These questions drive not only ancient but also modern discussions about free will, purpose, and meaning within the faith community.

The reverberations of this plural language extend beyond Genesis. It forms the foundation for thinking about community and mutual duty—not just with God but among people themselves. Church traditions and ethical systems often reference this shared origin as the wellspring of human responsibility to one another. When covenants form or communities gather to deliberate moral questions, they echo this primordial moment. The "let us make" of Genesis resonates whenever people pursue justice, mercy, or solidarity, reminding them that their story began within divine deliberation and continues as participants in an ongoing, plural conversation with God and each other.

Summary & Reflections of this Topic

Now that we have journeyed through the complex and rich meanings behind the plural language in **Genesis 1:26**, we can appreciate how this brief but profound phrase invites us to rethink God's nature and humanity's special place in creation. Whether seen as a **divine council** or a hint of the **Trinity**, the *"Let us make man in our image"* moment challenges us to recognize a <u>divine community at work</u>—a community that calls humans into **relationship, purpose, and responsibility**. This understanding encourages deeper reflection on what it means to be made in **<u>God's likeness</u>**, not just as individuals but as <u>beings connected to a larger, sacred story</u>. Moving forward, this insight can shape how we view human dignity, ethical living, and our shared destiny, inspiring us <u>to live in harmony with others</u> and <u>with the divine</u>, **<u>fully aware of the mystery and wonder embedded in our origin.</u>**

Chapter 3:

Rare 'Two ELEMENTS'; In Adam

What & How?

The Components of A HUMAN BEING

(GENESIS 2:7) "Then The LORD God *formed* man of 'dust' *from the ground*, and 'breathed' *into his nostril* the 'breath' *of life*; and man became a *living being*."

From "<u>Dust and Breath</u>": The Double Mystery of Adam's Creation

Long before questions about who we are and where we come from stirred human minds, a quiet moment unfolded in the earliest story of creation: a figure shaped from dust, given life through the breath of something beyond the earthly realm. This scene has puzzled thinkers for centuries, inviting them to wonder about what it means to be human. Is our essence bound to the soil beneath our feet, or does an unseen force within us reach toward something higher? The story raises more than curiosity—it opens a door to deep reflection on life, death, and the mystery that lies between body and spirit. As we step into this chapter, we find ourselves at the crossroads of ancient wisdom and ongoing debate, where simple words carry profound questions that continue to challenge, and inspire those seeking to understand the nature of humanity.

Possibility of Interpretation 1:

The <u>Dual Nature</u> of Humanity: <u>*Dust* and Divine *Breath*</u>

*"Then the LORD God formed the man of **dust** from the ground and breathed into his nostrils the **breath** of life."* **(Genesis 2:7)** stands at the heart of any biblical discussion about human nature. This powerful statement shows a striking scene: <u>humanity molded</u> from the humble **substance of earth**, then **animated** <u>by a deliberate, intimate divine action</u>. The verse departs from ancient mythologies where humans emerge from violence, cosmic accidents, or the bodies of defeated gods. Instead, Genesis presents creation as a personal, hands-on gesture by the divine, inscribing upon human beings both dignity and dependence.

In the context of ancient Near Eastern myths, this deliberate divine formation and breathing; are rare. Many stories from neighboring cultures, like the Babylonian Enuma Elish, describe humans as the afterthought of cosmic struggle—constructed to serve gods or sprung from chaos. **Genesis 2:7** sets God apart as a craftsman, kneeling in the dust, shaping a single life and then investing it with spirit. This unique portrayal suggests that **every human** carries the imprint of both the earth and the breath of divinity, anchoring doctrines of human worth, responsibility, and spiritual vocation.

Interpretations hinge on the two substances mentioned: "dust from the ground" (Clay/Dirt/Soil) and "the *breath of life (*Breathing energy from God Himself)." Physicalist readings underscore the significance of dust. Humans are, in this view, profoundly linked to the material world. The chemistry of the body mirrors the composition of soil—(carbon, calcium, iron, water…etc.)—revealing continuity with plants, animals, and the landscape itself. This earthy origin signals vulnerability and limitation. Religious traditions often echo this humility. Ash Wednesday (among the Christian Catholic community), marks foreheads of their fellowship on 'Hloy Friday' with ashes and proclaims, ***"You are dust, and to dust you shall return."*** Such rituals (in some way), teach awareness of mortality and foster reverence for the natural world.

A physicalist interpretation also fuels ethical discussions about humanity's responsibilities. When humans are seen as creatures of dust, their kinship with other forms of life becomes clear. This perspective underpins ecological ethics, arguing for care and humility toward the earth and other beings. For example, stewardship teachings in Judaism and Christianity urge people to look after the creation they came from, since to exploit the world recklessly is to disrespect their own deepest origins. Some theological voices insist that care for the earth is inseparable from faithfulness to God, because God is the one who formed people from the very materials they are called to protect.

Other interpreters focus on the "breath of life" as the definitive marker of humanity. <u>This divine breath distinguishes humans from animals</u>, according to spiritualist viewpoints, by endowing them with <u>consciousness, **moral discernment,** creativity, and the yearning for higher things</u>. **The breath** is not merely <u>oxygen</u> but a **mysterious, sacred force**—often understood as the human **soul or spirit**. In Jewish liturgy, prayers speak of God who "restores souls to dead bodies." **Christian creeds** declare belief in "***The Holy Spirit***, <u>The Lord and giver of life</u>." For many, the sense of being animated from within by something greater—call it conscience, inspiration, or longing for the eternal—offers daily evidence of the divine presence.

The spiritualist reading often underlies teachings about the sacred dignity of each person. If a spark of divine breath animates all people, then all deserving respect and protection, regardless of status or strength. Some mystical traditions, such as Kabbalah and strands of Christian theology, go further, suggesting that humans straddle two worlds. Their "feet in the dust" are matched by their "minds in the heavens," generating endless reflection on identity and destiny.

The encounter between dust and breath ignites lasting debates. These contrasting interpretations have sparked disagreement: Are people fundamentally bodies animated by spirit, or spirits acting through bodies? Greek philosophers such as Plato described the body as the prison of the soul, while others, like Aristotle, viewed soul and body as one integrated reality. Christian theologians wrestled with whether resurrection would mean a physical or spiritual renewal. These questions persist in Islam, Judaism, and modern secular philosophy, with doctrines such as the resurrection of the body, reincarnation, and even the debate over artificial intelligence and consciousness drawing on this foundational scriptural ambiguity.

This profound duality does not resolve into simple answers. Instead, it introduces a tension—between humility and hope, fragility and aspiration—that shapes every vision of mortality and immortality, and every search for the true seat of the human soul. Interpretations of **Genesis 2:7** continue to provoke thought about the limits of flesh, the reach of spirit, and mysteries that will compel generations to come.

Possibility of Interpretation 2:

Debating Mortality and Immortality: <u>Ancient and Modern Perspectives</u>

Humans first took shape from the dust of the earth, formed into being, then animated by the breath of God. This scene from Genesis 2:7 has puzzled generations, giving rise to fundamental questions about the nature of humanity. The debate turns on whether early humans were fated for mortality or designed for immortality.

One argument comes from a straightforward reading of the creation story. God shapes Adam from dust, a substance that returns to the earth. This view anchors humanity in the natural world, emphasizing physicality and finitude. The words spoken after the first act of disobedience—"for dust you are and to dust you will return" (Genesis 3:19)—have supported this view across traditions. **Scholars who favor this <u>interpretation point</u>** out that the Hebrew words for "soul" (nephesh) and "spirit" (ruach) often refer to life or breath rather than an immortal, detachable element. According to this approach, when the breath leaves the body, the person ceases to exist, echoing sentiments found in **Ecclesiastes 12:7**, where the <u>body returns to dust</u> and the <u>breath returns to God</u>.

In this tradition, death marks an end rather than a doorway. Human significance resides in the present, in the conduct and relationships that fill a finite existence. Cultures and philosophies influenced by this view have sometimes emphasized legacy, memory, and moral living as ways to bridge the gap between mortality and meaning. For some Jewish interpretations and strands of modern theology, there is little distinction between the "soul" and the totality of a living person, which aligns with physicalist philosophies that see consciousness and spirit as products of the body rather than separate, undying entities.

Against this, a contrasting view emerges from the focus on the divine breath. Some traditions—including ancient Christian, Orthodox, and Catholic teaching—have interpreted the breathing of God's spirit into Adam as a gift of immortality or an enduring soul. The act of animation does not merely grant biological life but bestows a spiritual essence, a capacity for ongoing relationship with the divine. This viewpoint finds support in theological traditions that argue for the soul as inherently immortal, a spark of divine image that cannot perish with the body. Early thinkers like Augustine and Thomas Aquinas taught that the soul survives physical death, awaiting future resurrection or reward.

Philosophers like Plato significantly influenced these spiritualist interpretations by teaching the soul's pre-existence and immortality. In "Phaedo," Plato presented death as a release for the soul, which belongs to a higher, eternal realm. These ideas flowed into Christian thought through figures such as Origen and were later integrated by Augustine, thus shaping doctrines that see each individual as a being of lasting significance, whose destiny stretches beyond the physical realm.

The Genesis text itself remains enigmatic, leaving space for both positions. The act of combining dust and breath can suggest a unity—body and spirit so interwoven that neither exists separately for long. The emergence of "a living soul" in Genesis 2:7 hints at an indivisible human, sustained by God's presence yet rooted in material form. This combination sets humanity apart from other creatures, introducing profound questions: Is the soul given in a single moment or developed over time? Was immortality a potential lost through the fall, or did mortality always define human borders?

These debates reach into larger theological questions. <u>Some traditions teach</u> that the soul was created to be immortal but was subjected to mortality due to disobedience. <u>Others maintain</u> that hope does not rest on a deathless soul but on God's promise to resurrect the entire person—body and breath reunited in a restoration of original intent. <u>Disagreements persist</u> about what ultimately becomes of the soul: endless life, eventual destruction, or transformation.

Beliefs about mortality and immortality echo through cultures and eras, shaping how people approach death and assign meaning to life. For those who see the soul as immortal, funerals and rituals often emphasize passage and reunion, framing death as a beginning as much as an end. For those who hold to an end-of-life view, the focus shifts to legacy, memory, and the ethical obligations of this present world. Both perspectives inspire deep moral reflection, leading individuals and societies to wrestle with questions of purpose, value, and hope.

The interplay of dust and breath in the Genesis story continues to invite inquiry. Its ambiguity fuels lively debates and personal reflection, encouraging an engagement with the deepest mysteries of human nature and destiny.

Summary & Reflections of this Topic

Now that we have explored the rich and complex duality embedded in **Genesis 2:7**—the blending of **dust** and **divine breath**—we are better equipped to appreciate the depth of <u>human nature as both physical and spiritual</u>. This chapter has shown how this ancient text invites ongoing reflection and debate about who we are, where we come from, and what awaits beyond life. Understanding these perspectives helps us engage thoughtfully with questions of <u>mortality, immortality</u>, and <u>identity</u>, encouraging us to carry forward insights from scripture into our own beliefs, values, and actions. By **embracing the mystery** and tension between <u>body and spirit</u>, we open ourselves to richer conversations about <u>faith, purpose, and the enduring search for meaning</u> in a world shaped by both earth and breath.

José E. Espinoza

Chapter 4:

Strange 'NAKEDNESS'! not Ashamed!

When? & Why?

(GENESIS 2:25) *"And the man and his wife were both 'naked' and were 'not ashamed".*

Innocence Revealed: Nakedness Without Shame

Nakedness is often seen today as something to hide or protect, a source of embarrassment or vulnerability. Imagine a time when it was nothing more than a natural state, free from judgment or fear. Picture two people living without any thought of shame or modesty, where clothes were not symbols of status or concealment but simply unnecessary. This image challenges everything we think we know about how humans relate to their own bodies and to one another. The discomfort we feel at exposure, the rules woven around clothing and privacy, all point to a deeper story—one that begins long before our modern ideas took shape. What happened in that first moment when nakedness stopped being just a fact of life and became a cause for hiding? The answers lie in an ancient world where innocence and awareness walked a delicate line, shaping how humanity understands itself even now.

José E. Espinoza

The Phenomenon of <u>Unashamed Nakedness</u>

Possibility of Interpretation 1:

In the earliest chapters of Genesis, the experience of nakedness among the first humans is a striking portrayal of innocence. These individuals lived <u>without the knowledge of good and evil</u>. Such knowledge had not yet entered their awareness, so there was no internal concept of right or wrong. Nakedness, for them, simply existed; it carried neither the label of virtue nor the stain of impropriety. Their bodies presented no reason for internal alarm, concern, or pride, for no cultural or ethical systems had been established to define or police bodily presentation. Social and religious taboos surrounding the exposure of the human body simply did not exist at that point. Without any internalized standard, Adam and Eve did not judge themselves, and nakedness could not become a source of awkwardness or shame.

This absolute neutrality may be challenging to grasp from a modern perspective, where clothing and bodily privacy have become deeply bound to notions of dignity, modesty, and even morality itself. But in the world as Genesis describes it, their bodies carried no narrative of embarrassment. Nothing about their form or presence could be considered inappropriate, shocking, or even noteworthy. Early humans did not compare themselves to others or hold themselves up against ideals. The condition of being nude was neither an act to be celebrated nor a state to be concealed; it was simply a feature of existence, as unremarkable as their own breathing.

Physically, their bodies reflected the creative purpose of their Maker. In the sacred narrative, humanity emerges as a direct expression of divine intent. Every limb, curve, and feature represented a wholeness unmarred by ailment or imperfection. No scars, blemishes, or weaknesses marred their skin. This unblemished physical state radiated not the unattainable standards of later generations, but the actual spiritual and material reality given to them in creation. Their forms did not mark social ranking or imply shameful difference; every finger, every line, every surface was simply good. The body itself was a vessel of beauty, crafted through loving invention, and its exposure did not invite ridicule or secrecy.

Possibility of Interpretation 2:

Imagine standing in a garden filled with every good thing to touch, taste, and see, where there is no voice calling you to hide, apologize, or correct. The fresh air brushes across your skin, and there is no impulse to cover or defend. In this setting, the body rests, free from threat and fear, not because of ignorance, but because no standard of judgment has been introduced. In a modern analogy, it can be compared to the freedom of a small child playing in the open, unconcerned by the conventions that later shape adult behavior and attitudes about the body, free yet unaware that "exposure" is something that could ever be thought of as negative.

Relationships among these first humans flourished in this soil of innocence. Physical nakedness matched a spiritual openness; there was no need for hidden motives or secrets. Their interactions were marked by trust and candor. Communication needed no filters or veils. Adam and Eve experienced a transparency with each other that found its mirror in their relationship with God. The absence of clothing was therefore not just a lack of fabric, but the outward sign of a community where barriers of suspicion, fear, and concealment simply did not exist. This sense of openness forged a deeper harmony, one where differences and vulnerabilities were not seen as matters to conceal, but simply as facts of being. There was unity and closeness—a deep solidarity—born from knowing oneself and being known, without threat or pretense.

Self-consciousness and the impulses of judgment were foreign to them. Embarrassment did not trouble their minds. No part of themselves or their world evoked a negative reaction or urge to withdraw. The absence of shame created space for tranquility. Their daily encounters were untouched by anxiety. There were no sidelong glances, no fears of rejection or inadequacy, and no longing to measure up to a hidden ideal. Acceptance of self—of the body—was as natural as breathing. This environment fostered peaceful assurance, with no storm of doubts or inner criticism.

Yet lurking beneath this purity of experience was the possibility of change. <u>Neutrality and innocence unsettled only</u> **by the distant shadow of a new knowledge,** a knowledge that would one day introduce questions and unsettle this profound serenity. The narrative hints that innocence, while beautiful, was not unassailable. The stage was quietly being set for an encounter that would transform everything, floating just beyond the edge of that primordial peace.

Summary & Reflections of this Topic

Understanding the original state of unashamed nakedness in early humans and the profound transformation that followed the fall offers us valuable insight into the roots of modesty, shame, and social norms. This chapter shows how innocence once allowed for complete openness—physically, emotionally, and spiritually—free from judgment or fear. Yet, with the emergence of self-awareness came a new reality marked by vulnerability and the need to protect oneself. Now that we have explored this pivotal shift, we can better appreciate the lasting impact these changes have on human relationships, cultural practices, and our ongoing search for dignity and trust. Recognizing this foundation invites us to reflect on how notions of shame and modesty continue to shape our lives today and challenges us to approach these themes with deeper understanding and compassion.

Chapter 5:

Mysterious 'SERPENT'! &

'Controversy'

How & why?

(GENESIS 3:1-5) *"… the 'serpent' was more crafty than any beast … which the Lord God had made…"*

A Talking Tempter: The Serpent's Shocking Role

"You will not certainly die," the serpent whispered, its words weaving doubt where none had been before. This simple conversation, unfolding in the garden's quiet stillness, marks a turning point that continues to fascinate and puzzle readers across centuries. The creature speaking to Eve was unlike any ordinary animal—it demonstrated cunning, intelligence, and a skillful use of language that challenges common assumptions about the nature of temptation and evil. Far from a mindless **beast**, this serpent engages with thought, strategy, and ambiguity, raising profound questions about identity and purpose within the earliest story of humanity's fall. What motives lie behind its words? Is it merely a creature, a symbol, or something more? As we explore these questions, the serpent emerges not just as a character in an ancient tale but as a figure whose mystery invites us to reconsider the origins of doubt, choice, and consequence in human experience.

José E. Espinoza

Possibility of Interpretation 1:

The <u>Serpent's Character</u>: Intelligence, Speech, and Identity

Genesis 3:1–5 presents an exchange distinctly different from anything else in the opening chapters. The serpent's entrance onto the stage involves not mere presence but active engagement with language and thought. The text highlights this from the start: ***"Now the serpent was <u>more crafty</u> than any of the <u>wild animals of the field wich the Lord God had made</u>."*** This claim establishes the serpent's <u>advanced mental faculties</u>, marking it as an outlier among creatures. Unlike typical animals, which act on instinct and lack self-conscious reasoning in scriptural narratives, <u>this being initiates a structured, nuanced conversation with Eve</u>.

Language in **Genesis 3: 1-5** is not used by the serpent in simple or accidental ways. The serpent frames its initial inquiry carefully: ***"Did God really say, 'You must not eat from any tree in the garden'?"*** **(Genesis 3:1, NIV).** The wording is both pointed and ambiguous, using a question that appears innocent while subtly exaggerating the prohibition. The serpent does not issue a direct command or make an outright false claim but rather uses language to sow seeds of doubt, tapping into Eve's memory of God's words. Here, rhetorical skill is plainly visible. Rather than an animal driven by urge or hunger, the serpent demonstrates conscious strategy: it distorts, reframes, and invites reconsideration.

Far from acting as a dumb beast, the serpent's persuasion emerges through psychological tactics. It operates with implication and suggestion, forcing Eve to clarify and defend God's instructions. When Eve responds with, *"We may eat fruit from the trees in the garden, but God did say, 'You must not eat fruit from the tree that is in the middle of the garden, and you must not touch it, or you will die,'"* the serpent seizes the moment. Instead of simply denying the warning, the serpent replies, ***"You will not certainly die . . . For God knows that when you eat from it your eyes will be opened, and you will be like God, knowing good and evil"*** (Genesis 3:4-5). This response employs two interwoven strategies: first, **it challenges the notion of consequence by directly opposing God's warning**; second, it appeals to the promise of enlightenment. The argument is not rooted in brute denial but in persuasive, carefully constructed counter-narratives—an effort to reshape perception, not just erode obedience.

These techniques distinguish the serpent from any standard scriptural animal figure. Neither cattle nor birds, lions nor donkeys, engage in this manner. The only biblical parallel for a talking animal is Balaam's donkey, and there, the animal's speech is explicitly attributed to divine intervention. In Genesis 3, the narrator's silence about the source of the serpent's speech has fueled centuries of debate. Was it merely a clever creature with special powers, or did another force act through it? The identification of the serpent as Satan emerges in later scriptures like **Revelation 12:9 and 20:2,** where the terms *"serpent,"* "devil," and "satan" are linked. Most theological interpretations hold that ***satan** (*opponent or *obstructor), a spiritual being, either 'appeared in the strategic guise of a serpent', or 'possessed one', using its form as a vehicle for temptation.

José E. Espinoza

Possibility of Interpretation 2:

Some Traditional & Philosophical Ideas

Other traditions read the serpent as a symbol. Philo's allegory interprets the serpent as desire: a force able to flatter, distort, and bring harm under the guise of enjoyment. This interpretation transforms the episode into a meditation on the power of temptation and the psychological struggle between sense and pleasure. In the eyes of critics like Victor Hamilton, attempts to avoid the messianic dimension of this verse—where the serpent's offspring opposes the woman's—miss essential layers of meaning. The text's ambiguity allows for multiple readings, inviting each generation to wrestle with the same questions of evil, temptation, and deception.

Before the fall, nothing in Genesis identifies the **serpent as an enemy**. The narrative offers no hint of animosity or threat. Eve's willingness to stand and engage in conversation suggests a climate of openness or, at the least, no expectation of danger. God's creatures lived in harmony. Only after the conversation, and the subsequent disobedience, does God pronounce a curse: ***"I will put enmity between you and the woman, and between your offspring and hers"* (Genesis 3:15).** This transformation—from ambiguous presence to adversarial figure—profoundly alters later theological and literary treatments. In Jewish and Christian traditions alike, the serpent stands as the archetype of opposition: cunning, fallen, and separated from humanity by decree and destiny.

The serpent's speaking role remains a pivotal and **mysterious aspect** of Genesis. Its unique mixture of intellect, persuasive mastery, and symbolic ambiguity intensifies the drama of Eden. The layered debate about its identity and relationship with human beings continues to spark new interpretations, shaping an ever-evolving conversation on the origins of temptation, evil, and the persistent questions of motive and identity at the heart of the sacred story.

Possibility of Interpretation 3:

The <u>Serpent's Motives</u> and Aftermath: Instigating the Fall

The serpent in Genesis 3 stands apart as a **mysterious and cunning figure,** whose words and actions drive the narrative of the fall in profound ways. Previous exploration has shown its rare speech, rational agency, and uncertain identity set it apart from other creatures, raising the question of what truly prompted its intervention in the first place. Discussion of motive and method must reach into the depths of ancient context and diverse theological traditions.

A long-standing interpretation, especially prominent in later Jewish and Christian readings, presents the serpent as the embodiment of evil, sometimes aligning it directly with Satan. In this view, the temptation in Eden signals a decisive confrontation between the forces of God and those seeking to oppose Him. **Genesis 3:13-15** records God's words to the serpent, ***"I will put enmity between you and the woman, and between your offspring and hers; he will crush your head, and you will strike his heel."*** The direct placement of enmity has been widely read as an introduction of cosmic rivalry, framing the serpent not as an isolated deceiver but as a manifestation of a wider, ongoing struggle. The intellectual force and calculated speech of the serpent further reinforce the sense that its role is deliberate, deliberate and adversarial, far beyond mere animalistic instinct.

The serpent's alignment with broader evil gains additional significance through later traditions that reimagine the episode as humanity's first battle with Satan's guile. This interpretive move amplifies the gravity of the scene and transforms the serpent's temptation into a symbol of perennial opposition: humanity forever caught between the commands of God and the cunning deceptions that would pull it astray. This cosmic dimension of the serpent's motive positions it as an agent whose very purpose is to oppose God's order, seek the corruption of God's creation, and ensure the ongoing existence of evil and suffering in the world.

Yet competing perspectives have argued that reading the serpent simply as the devil may miss the layered complexity of the story's original setting. Some scholars propose the serpent acts as a test, either allowed or even appointed by divine will to probe the loyalty and maturity of early humanity. In this light, the narrative does not present the serpent as an external invader or supernatural villain, but as a device woven into creation, meant to provide Adam and Eve with a genuine opportunity to exercise free choice. The challenge issued by the serpent compels humanity to make a conscious decision, weighing obedience against the allure of autonomy and self-determination. Rather than representing evil as a cosmic intruder, the serpent becomes the catalyst through which humans acquire moral discernment; their choice speaks to their capacity for independent faithfulness or rebellion.

This reading reframes the serpent's role from pure opposition to provocative instrumentality. The test introduced in Eden is not merely destructive but necessary for the growth and integrity of free will. Without challenge, there can be no responsible virtue, and so the serpent's presence functions as an essential component in the development of genuine moral agency. Through this lens, God's apparent allowance of the serpent does not undermine divine goodness but affirms the importance of voluntary faith and accountability.

The serpent's principal method stems from psychological manipulation and the sowing of doubt. Rather than using force or direct coercion, the serpent approaches Eve with carefully crafted questions and subtly misleading assertions. **"Did God really say,** 'You must not eat from any tree in the garden'?" marks the beginning of the exchange, <u>planting the seed of uncertainty around God's words</u>. As the serpent and Eve converse, he challenges the directness of divine command, eventually asserting, "You will not certainly die… For God knows that when you eat from it your eyes will be opened, and <u>you will be like God</u>, **knowing** <u>good and **evil**</u>". By employing ambiguity, the serpent blurs the boundaries between truth and lie, enticing Adam and Eve to trust their <u>own reasoning over obedience</u>. This psychological tactic—undermining trust through doubt—powerfully reshapes their perception and disrupts the foundational relationship with God.

The aftermath of the serpent's actions reverberates beyond Eden. God's pronouncement of ongoing enmity between the serpent and the woman establishes a pattern of **perpetual conflict,** with later generations viewing this as emblematic of humanity's constant struggle against temptation and evil. The antagonism between the serpent's offspring and Eve's descendants comes to symbolize the lasting battle between virtue and vice, a motif echoed repeatedly in scripture and religious thought. The serpent is not confined to Genesis but emerges as a permanent adversary, a representation of the obstacles faced in every moral journey and spiritual pursuit.

Different traditions, while disagreeing on **the essence of the serpent's motivation**, recognize its role as an instigator whose actions permanently altered human destiny. Its methodical use of doubt, its ambiguous identification, and its enduring legacy as **spiritual opponent** ensure that the serpent remains central to ongoing discussions about evil, responsibility, and the challenges of moral growth.

Summary & Reflections of this Topic

Having examined the **serpent's** unique blend of **intelligence**, ambiguous **identity**, and psychological **tactics**, we now see it as more than a mere creature—it is a pivotal figure whose role challenges readers to reconsider the origins of temptation and moral choice. This understanding invites us to explore how the serpent's methods of doubt and persuasion continue to shape human experiences of temptation and ethical decision-making. With these insights, scholars, educators, and curious readers alike can approach the Eden narrative with renewed depth, using its complexities to inform broader discussions on free will, responsibility, and the enduring struggle between obedience and autonomy in the spiritual journey ahead.

Chapter 6:

Enigma of "the other Animals"

What? - Why?

The Strange Case of the Other Animals

(GENESIS 3:1) *"… was more crafty than any of the wild animals the Lord God had made. …"*

Animals of Eden: Minds and Speech, Plus the "Beast/Wild Animals of the Field"

Have you ever paused to consider how animals might have related to humans in the earliest moments of creation? Could these creatures in similitude such as the serpent in **Genesis 3:1** have possessed minds capable of speech and understanding, engaging with humanity in ways that challenge our modern assumptions? What changed in those relationships after the Fall, reshaping the nature of communication and connection between people and animals? And what we understand (in some translated bible version) by the remark; "...***more crafty*** than *"any **beast of the field...**"*, and in many others; "wild animals". Is this reference to the 'Garden of Eden territory'? **What Beasts/Wild Animal? And What Field** does the Bible refers here? This chapter invites you to explore these questions by examining the fascinating possibility that the Garden of Eden was a place where animals and humans shared more than mere coexistence—they may have shared intellect, language, and a deep spiritual partnership. By looking closely at the biblical text and its descriptions of the ***"beasts of the field, or wild animal"*** we can gain fresh insights into an ancient world where boundaries between species were not yet fixed, opening a window into a lost harmony and the profound shifts that followed.

Possibility of Interpretation 1:

(Beasts/Animals)

Animal Intelligence, Speech, and <u>Relationships in Eden</u>

In the account of **Genesis 3:1**, the serpent's <u>ability to communicate</u> with Eve is presented without any suggestion of surprise or alarm from either human. **Eve converses naturally with the serpent**, which raises intriguing questions about the expectations of <u>animal intelligence and speech in Eden's earliest days</u>. When the text introduces a talking animal, it does not frame this event as extraordinary; instead, the focus is on the content of the conversation and the choices being made. This absence of shock hints that some level of animal communication may have been normal for both Adam and Eve. Interactions between human and animal might have occurred in a way that allowed ideas, intentions, or even spoken words to be clearly exchanged, suggesting Eden was a place where advanced cognition and mutual understanding were hallmarks of life.

Scripture's silence about any astonishment in this case, further bolsters the proposal that animals could possess highly developed communication skills, or even a <u>primitive form of language</u>. And it is presented in this portion of the bible, as something normal in this environment. The narrative, therefore, leaves room to imagine that **Eden's creatures**—perhaps especially those termed <u>"beasts of the field or wild animals"</u>—enjoyed mental and communicative <u>abilities beyond what modern experience</u> would allow. The presence of the serpent as a speaking being frames a broader possibility that other animals too might have shared in these gifts. Just as Eve perceived the serpent's statement as something to evaluate and discuss, rather than react to with confusion or fear, such interactions appear to take place against a backdrop of mutual comprehension.

José E. Espinoza

Spiritual Communion in Eden

Before the entrance of sin, Eden would have been marked by a sense of profound unity between all living beings. Instead of division or suspicion, the reality of the Garden involved humans and animals cooperating in a shared purpose. The human calling to "work and keep" the garden was not simply a one-sided management of resources; it might had required a partnership between Adam, Eve, and the animals. **Imagining** this harmony invites the reconstruction of scenes where, **for example**; Adam names each animal not as a master over slaves, but in an **act of partnership recognition** due to character, unique ability, purpose, and friendship. He meets a lion, regards its clear golden eyes, and speaks a name that fits its strength and gentleness. The lion in turn sits near, unafraid and attentive, trusting the human's judgment. In another corner, a pair of birds sings not just for themselves but perhaps in ways that offer guidance to Adam.

Instead of isolated creatures, the animals in Eden may have served as active participants in tending to the needs of the Garden. An elephant might purposefully uproot a heavy branch and bring it close. No fear, no confusion—every movement holds meaning, every action is a thread in the larger tapestry of stewardship. These possible scenes allow for an Eden in which every creature contributes to order, beauty, and abundance, all within a climate of implicit trust.

Stewardship and the Ideal Order

The relationship between humans and animals differs substantially from any notion of domination. **Stewardship means responsibility on behalf of another's well-being**. Unlike domination, which is based on using power to control or exploit, stewardship in Eden is more like the gentle guidance of a gardener tending delicate plants. Adam cares for each creature, not because he has the right to force obedience, but because it is in his nature to nurture and protect. Both animals and humans are dependent on one another and on the environment, their mutual dependence forming a sacred bond. This vision stands in contrast to power hierarchies; rather than separating humans and animals by insurmountable boundaries, it unites them in a participatory order—a community of **agents** working toward the flourishing of all members of Eden.

Possibility of Interpretation 2:

(All the rest of the Animals)

The Fracture After the Fall

With the entrance of sin and the issuance of the curse, everything changes. Genesis records that Adam and Eve's expulsion from the Garden is accompanied by a new reality of pain, resistance, and conflict between living things. Where once animals might have met the human gaze with trust, now suspicion and fear can invade their minds. **Speech and mutual understanding**, if they once existed between animals and people, disappear. The serpent's unique role in the Fall marks the beginning of new boundaries; from this moment, animals become "other." Communication narrows, animal consciousness may dim, and the potential for violence and distrust begins to poison relationships that were once harmonious.

Instead of gardeners and helpers, the creatures of the world are now **objects of struggle**. Thorns, thistles, and predatory behaviors emerge in the natural order. The scriptural picture that follows the Fall is shaped by estrangement and the reality of suffering in all creatures, separation, and death. The special case of the serpent, *"cursed among all animals/beasts of the field"* (Genesis 3:14), is the first in a long history of boundaries that will now define the new order of creation. Questions remain about the distinctions between the **various *"beasts of the field or wild animals,"*** setting the stage for further exploration of animal differentiation in a world marked by both continuity and loss.

The 'Beast of the Field/Any Other Animal' & the Uniqueness of the Serpent

Possibility of Interpretation 1:

(*Beast/*Wild Animal…)

The early chapters of Genesis depict a world where relationships between humans and animals reflect harmony and a shared stewardship. Animals in Eden live alongside humans as companions with apparent intelligence, and the story often suggests an order where understanding and cooperation are part of the original design. As the narrative turns to the serpent in **Genesis 3:1**, the term *"beast of the field"* or in other versions *"wild animal"* emerges with particular importance. Among all the creatures, the serpent stands apart, described as **"more crafty** *than any **Beast/Animal** that the Lord God had made."* This single phrase reveals an evident hierarchy, signaling an intellectual and perhaps spiritual quality unique to the serpent, drawing interest to its precise role and nature in the events that unfold.

The **Hebrew term** for serpent, **"nachash,"** signals more than mere physical difference. It emphasizes a <u>creature with capabilities exceeding those of its peers</u>. The biblical use of **"crafty" (arum)** suggests <u>intentional, calculated thought</u>, not simply animal cunning. Some traditional scholars hold that this craftiness represents an elevated reasoning ability—perhaps even speech—that distinguished the serpent from every other animal. Scriptural details reinforce this: in the Eden narrative, Eve holds a conversation with the serpent, which not only articulates complex ideas but challenges divine instruction, a task not attributed to any other creature in the garden.

Debate over the **serpent's true identity** and abilities has spanned centuries. Classical readings, viewing the Genesis narrative as historical, accept the <u>serpent as an animal</u>, albeit a remarkably gifted one, possibly endowed with the ability to speak and reason for purposes of the story. Some later interpretations, influenced by the development of biblical demonology, introduce a layer of spiritual intrigue. The <u>suggestion that</u> <u>satan acted through the serpent</u> becomes prominent in early Christian commentary, drawing lines from **Genesis 3** to New Testament passages where the serpent and satan are connected (**Revelation 12:9; 20:2; Mark 1:13**). However, as Dolansky emphasizes, there is no unambiguous biblical passage directly equating the Edenic serpent with satan; rather, the association develops over time through interpretation and tradition.

The New Testament provides moments of comparison, such as **Mark 1:13,** which presents **Jesus among <u>"the wild animals/ *beasts"</u>** and attended by angels after his temptation by satan. Here, animals appear in a spiritualized context, but the narrative separates their presence from the actions of satan, suggesting potential for animals to serve as both literal companions and as figures with possible spiritual significance that never quite blends into demonic agency. Unlike this broader use, **Genesis 3:1** (in many translations), makes a uniquely explicit point about the serpent's singular status among Edenic fauna, using "**<u>field</u>**" as a defining context. <u>The phrase</u> *"beasts of the <u>field</u>," (or Wild Animals in other versions),* may refer not only to ordinary animals but to a subset with <u>specific intellectual or functional traits</u>. Some readings of the text even explore whether such "beasts" or "wild animals", included <u>creatures with more advanced physiology</u>, 'such as upright posture or articulate speech', adding further weight to the serpent's distinctiveness.

The aftermath of the Fall intensifies these distinctions. The curse upon the serpent results in profound alteration: from an upright creature with gifted intellect, the serpent is consigned to crawl ***"on your belly,"*** <u>marking physical transformation</u> and a permanent lowering of status. The curse's language also introduces symbolic boundaries, declaring enmity between the serpent and the woman's seed—a break that echoes through human-animal relationships and theological symbolism for centuries. The text in Genesis 3:14 notes, ***"cursed are you above all <u>livestock</u> and all <u>wild animals</u>," "And more than every <u>beast of the field</u>"***... suggesting the serpent's new and lasting separation from its fellow creatures. Still, the narrative preserves the serpent's status as an illustrative figure, embodying both the literal and symbolic consequences of rebellion and divine judgment.

These story elements reveal a shift not only in the relationship between humans and a now-accursed animal but also in the broader order of creation. The separation imposed after the Fall serves as a defining moment for animal-human interaction and the theological imagination that grows from it. The serpent's **special craftiness, once an asset, becomes the reason for its distinction and punishment.** Through language, role, and consequence, Genesis crafts a layered narrative about boundaries, responsibilities, and the changed nature of the world—a world where animal intelligence and partnership become marred by the memory of **paradise lost** and by the hardships and suspicions to follow.

José E. Espinoza

Summary & Reflections of this Chapter

Understanding the unique nature of animal intelligence and communication in Eden opens new paths for interpreting the early biblical narrative, inviting us to reconsider how humans once related to the creatures around them—not as distant masters, but as partners in a shared harmony. Recognizing as well, the mystery/enigma of the _**"other animals" or "beasts of the field,"**_ and the serpent's distinct role, challenges us <u>to explore the deeper</u> spiritual and theological meanings beneath the surface of the text, encouraging fresh dialogue about the boundaries and relationships shaped by the Fall. With these insights, we can approach Scripture with renewed curiosity, ready to examine how the original unity between humans and animals informs broader themes of stewardship, trust, and loss, enriching both scholarly study and teaching while inspiring thoughtful reflection on our place within creation today. At the same time, keeping in mind that there is a <u>possibility of differences; between the commonly known animals and the **"beasts** of the **field" or "wild animals"**</u>.

Chapter 7:

Strange '<u>FRUIT</u>'! & '<u>Lethal</u>'

Which one? & Why?

(GENESIS 3:6-7) *"… the tree was desirable to make one 'wise,' <u>she took from its fruit</u> and ate; and she gave …"*

<u>Strange Fruit</u>, Tragic, Catastrophic & Unknown

José E. Espinoza

The Forbidden & Mysterious <u>Fruit</u>: (Genesis 3:6,7). Unmasking the Unknown Fruit/Tree

"She took of its fruit and ate, and she also gave some to her husband who was with her, and he ate." This simple sentence from Genesis has echoed through centuries, capturing imaginations and raising questions that have never fully been answered. **What exactly was this fruit?** <u>Why does the text leave it unnamed?</u> The silence around its identity invites endless speculation, not only about the story itself but about the nature of knowledge, choice, and consequence. Across cultures and generations, the fruit has become a symbol—sometimes an apple, other times something entirely different—each interpretation reflecting more about those who tell the story than the story alone. As we delve into this mystery, we uncover how the unknown fruit shapes our understanding of humanity's first steps toward awareness, responsibility, and the complex relationship between innocence and experience.

Possibility of Interpretation 1:

Decoding the <u>Unnamed Fruit</u>: Interpretations and Significance

***"She took of its fruit and ate, and she also gave some to her husband who was with her, and he ate"* (Genesis 3:6)** stands as one of the most echoed moments in biblical literature. The act described in Genesis marks the emergence of disobedience as a turning point for humanity. Yet, the fruit at the heart of this pivotal event remains unnamed and undefined. The original Hebrew text offers no clarification about what type of fruit was consumed. From the very first retelling, this absence creates an intentional silence. It introduces an air of mystery that refuses simple answers, inviting questions about both the story itself and the way meaning is constructed within sacred texts.

Literal interpretations seek to answer this silence. Western culture often presents the fruit as an apple. Many artists painted Eve holding or biting an apple; these images appear in stained glass, sculpture, and Renaissance masterpieces. In Latin, the <u>word for "apple" and "evil"</u> <u>(malum)</u> share a root, which may have shaped medieval interpretations and thus Western doctrine. Over time, this association made the apple a powerful emblem for temptation and sin, **even though the <u>original text makes no mention of apples</u>**. The apple, therefore, is less a scriptural certainty and more an example of how interpretation grows into tradition.

Alternative literal theories challenge the apple's dominance. Some readers argue that the fruit was most likely a fig, turning to the biblical detail that Adam and Eve, once aware of their nakedness, used fig leaves to cover themselves soon after eating from the tree. The close textual and physical relationship between the tree, the fruit, and the fig leaves sparks this possibility. Others propose the fruit as a pomegranate, noting the fruit's rich symbolism in ancient Near Eastern cultures; pomegranates, packed with seeds, symbolize fertility and abundance. Grapes have also entered the discussion, in part because of their links to wine and intoxication in both biblical and extra-biblical mythologies. Each of these ideas points to influences outside the original text, relying on symbolism prevalent in nearby cultures or on clues in later verses.

Possibility of Interpretation 2:

Commentaries & Allegories

Allegorical interpretations step beyond the literal fruit. Some commentators see the fruit as a metaphor for the act of acquiring forbidden or experiential knowledge—an invitation to think about learning beyond prescribed limits. Eating the fruit represents a conscious crossing from innocence into self-awareness. It is a step that forever changes the relationship between humanity and the divine. This act may signify the birth of conscience or the origin of moral dilemma. Many thinkers view the fruit as a symbol for the human desire to know and understand, even when such understanding brings suffering or loss.

Within theological and mythological studies, interpreters have suggested that the fruit stands in for new desires and moral intricacies. For some, it signifies sexual awakening, as the newfound awareness leads Adam and Eve to notice and cover their bodies. Others connect the fruit to intellectual curiosity, where the pursuit of knowledge becomes a double-edged sword, sparking enlightenment but leading to alienation. The fruit, then, is not simply food or substance, but the threshold into human maturity, responsibility, and the capacity to make choices with lasting consequences.

The crowning element in the story is the text's refusal to define the fruit. This silence has purpose. It gives the story lasting relevance by requiring interpretation. Every culture and generation bring new questions and answers: each approaches the fragment with cultural assumptions about knowledge, authority, and transgression. Instead of closing down discussion, the ambiguity asks readers to fill in the gap. The lack of specificity means that the fruit becomes a mirror for the reader's own fears and hopes about the unknown. This openness is essential to why the narrative endures as a source for debate and inspiration.

Subtly, the unresolved nature of the fruit's identity forces the audience to wrestle with not just what happened in Eden, but also why it happened and why that mystery matters. As the story stands, it draws attention to much larger questions about the risks and rewards of seeking understanding. The ambiguity at the center of Genesis 3:6, instead of weakening the story, becomes its greatest strength. It leaves space for readers to reflect on knowledge, consequence, and the endless search for meaning within a world shaped by choices—inviting echoing questions about enlightenment and human responsibility.

<u>Another</u> Possibility of Interpretation:

Aftermath and Meaning: *Consequences of Consuming the Fruit

Ambiguity in the Genesis account of the Tree of Knowledge gives readers space for interpretation and ongoing reflection. This purposeful vagueness encourages both ancient and modern thinkers to constantly revisit the text, interrogating the meaning and repercussions of eating the fruit. The ambiguity also frames the knowledge gained as potentially enlightening or condemning, sparking wide-ranging debates about human autonomy, existential suffering, and the limits of ethical action.

Interpretative frameworks develop along two main lines: some view the event as a necessary catalyst for human growth, while others see it as the beginning of a tragic estrangement from original innocence. In the first framework, the act of eating the fruit marks the awakening of moral self-awareness. Humanity, in this telling, transitions from passive obedience to active agency. Some theologians interpret the acquisition of knowledge as an intended step on the path to maturity, rather than a simple act of rebellion. This framework can be traced to traditions that highlight the value of free will. In these readings, knowledge and discernment are necessary for genuine relationship with the divine, not merely for the fulfillment of one's own desires.

This tradition finds echoes in the writing of figures who argue that knowledge is both a blessing and a burden. Gaining it requires the risk of defying conventional limitations, but it also opens new avenues for wisdom, responsibility, and grace. Certain Church Fathers, for example, speculate that the divine plan always included the potential for growth, understanding, and reconciliation—Irenaeus famously characterized the initial act as part of a developmental process, comparing humanity to children destined to mature into full moral agents. Doctrinal interpretations within some Protestant circles argue that knowledge of good and evil, though costly, is also tied to human dignity and reflects the image of God within each person.

The opposing view interprets the act as forbidden—an overreaching grasp for divine prerogative. Commentaries from Augustine to many medieval theologians often depict the eating of the fruit as rebellion and pride, resulting in estrangement, suffering, and a fractured creation. In this perspective, knowledge brings existential sorrow. Alienation from God and loss of innocence dominate. Humanity is portrayed as turning away from rightful obedience, shattering harmony with nature and opening the path toward the necessity of redemption. The connection between this perceived hubris and the environmental crisis, for instance, appears in critiques that trace harmful instrumental attitudes toward nature to anthropocentric readings of Genesis, which suggest humans are entitled to exploit creation for their benefit.

The debate between these frameworks shapes doctrines of free will, obedience, and redemption. Traditions that frame the fruit as part of maturation may emphasize God's desire for humans with agency, suggesting that moral choice and the possibility of grace only emerge when knowledge makes genuine decisions possible. Augustine and his followers, in contrast, see the will's misuse as necessitating divine intervention and redemption, interpreting the story as humanity's need for boundaries and the consequences of stepping beyond them.

Responsibility and the process of growth become central questions in readings of Genesis. Some thinkers ask whether wisdom can be gained only through experience, often transgressive or painful. The fruit's allure represents not only the promise of enlightenment but also the dangers that come with unchecked ambition. The story thus dramatizes the moral tension between curiosity and trust, between the pursuit of knowledge and the cost of lost innocence. In some traditions, "innocence" is idealized as purity and simple trust. In others, innocence gives way to the necessity of grappling with complexity; only through struggle and even error can one reach true maturity or moral depth.

The relationship between innocence and maturity is continually reimagined. In certain philosophical and theological schools, maturing involves wrestling with ambiguity and accepting one's responsibilities—even the burden of knowledge that can never be completely put aside. Some commentators argue that a passive or naïve innocence is unsustainable, while others mourn what is lost when innocence yields to worldly experience. This ongoing tension shapes not only how individuals are seen but also the evolution of theological and ethical paradigms.

José E. Espinoza

Ongoing re-evaluation of the Genesis account also mirrors contemporary concerns: the instrumental versus intrinsic value of nature, human responsibility for ecological consequences, and the limitations of anthropocentrism. The story's dual emphasis—on possibility and danger, growth and loss—unlocks paradigm shifts that influence doctrine and practice, prompting renewed attention to questions of autonomy, obedience, and the ethics of knowledge itself. Through this ever-evolving conversation, the fruit continues to symbolize both the perils and the promise of human striving.

Summary & Reflections on this Topic

Now that we have explored the many layers surrounding the Tree of Knowledge's fruit—from its elusive identity to the profound consequences of its consumption—we can appreciate how this ancient story continues to challenge and inspire us. Its deliberate ambiguity invites each generation to engage with enduring questions about knowledge, choice, and responsibility, encouraging us to reflect on our own journeys between innocence and understanding. As we move forward, this chapter lays the foundation for deeper exploration into how these themes shape not only theological thought but also our personal and collective search for meaning in a complex world.

José E. Espinoza

Part 2:

Different Era

Rebellion, Independence, & Autocracy of Humanity

Chapter 8:

Enigma of the 'FIG's LEAVES'

Why? Who's Idea?

(GENESIS 3:7)

"… And they knew that they were naked; and <u>they sewed fig leaves</u> together <u>and made</u> themselves <u>loin coverings.</u>"

José E. Espinoza

Fig's Leaves and Fruited Realities

"Where can we find something to cover ourselves?" (Adam might have asked, or perhaps Eve). The simplicity of the question hides a profound moment—an awakening to vulnerability, shame, and the desperate search for security. What begins as a matter of physical covering soon reveals layers of meaning tied to human nature, trust, and the choices that shape our existence. This tension between what is seen and what lies beneath invites us to look deeper into the symbols woven quietly into the story—the leaves, the fruit, and the silence that surrounds them. Through this lens, we uncover not only ancient customs and cultural significance but also timeless questions about obedience, temptation, and the ways people respond when faced with the unknown. As we journey through these themes, we are reminded that sometimes what remains unnamed holds the greatest power to speak across time and touch the heart of every reader.

Possibility of Interpretation 1:

The Specificity of <u>Figs</u> in the Narrative

Within this landscape, the Genesis narrative's choice of figs as the first source for covering takes on subtle resonance. The natural abundance of fig trees in the warm Mediterranean climate, especially near ancient settlements, made their leaves immediately accessible to Adam and Eve in their hour of need. Fig trees thrive in the rocky soils of this region, their roots reaching deep and their branches casting broad, cool shade on the outskirts of villages. One can imagine the scene: the dense, gnarled tree offering not only fruit for the hungry but also wide, fleecy leaves large enough to be fashioned into rudimentary garments. Their distinctive lobed shape and supple texture, compared with the smaller, tougher leaves of olive or acacia, made fig leaves an obvious and practical solution for desperate hands. This immediate accessibility is more than a botanical detail—it reveals how quickly Adam and Eve responded to newfound vulnerability, grasping the nearest suitable covering in an instinctive effort to shield their shame. The tangible reality of these broad leaves amplifies the sense of urgency and agency in the story, demonstrating how human beings act decisively in moments of existential crisis.

This motif of fragile coverings recurs in biblical literature. In the prophetic era, Israel's reliance on external religious observance—ritual sacrifices or festivals—without heartfelt repentance carries a similar sense of insufficiency. The prophet Isaiah, for example, chastised the people for drawing near with their lips while their hearts remained distant, exposing the superficiality of ritual without genuine transformation. The fig leaves of Eden, then, gesture to a universal pattern: the use of fleeting, ultimately hollow means to cope with shame and guilt, a tension resolved not by human initiative but by the patient, lasting work of divine grace.

Across the Scriptures, the symbolic power of figs expands further, coming to serve as a barometer for the spiritual health of God's people. Prophets and poets alike describe those blessed as "sitting under their vine and fig tree," a phrase expressing peace, provision, and security under God's favor. Jeremiah's vision of good and bad figs distinguishes the faithful remnant from the corrupt, forecasting both hope and doom. Even Jesus draws on this motif, cursing a fruitless fig tree to illustrate the perils of outward piety devoid of true righteousness and warning Jerusalem of its impending desolation.

Possibility of Interpretation 2:

Fig vs Fruit of Disobedience: Ambiguity and Its Implications

The **fig tree,** so familiar in the ancient region, (and <u>mostly anywhere</u> in the soil of the world), compared to the unknown forbidden fruit, stands as far more than **a simple plant** in the Genesis narrative. It emerges in the moment Adam and Eve attempt to cover their nakedness, <u>shaping the **fig leaf** into a symbol of sudden awareness and shame</u>. This detail draws readers into the complicated world of human guilt and the drive to conceal wrongdoing. Yet, as **attention lingers on the fig leaves,** <u>not in the fruit</u>! Neider on the fig tree itself! the story quietly introduces another puzzle—the fruit itself. Remarking the point on the purpose Adam and Eve used these fig's leaves. And at the same time, we must keep in mind that <u>there was not warning or concern about the fig</u> <u>fruit</u>, in comparison to the 'fruit from the tree of knowledge of good and evil'. Unlike the fig, this pivotal object of temptation refuses clear description or identification. The narrator withholds its name, and this lack of detail is intentional, casting a veil of ambiguity over the central act of disobedience.

Yet, in remark of the fig's leaves, as an instrument of immediate resource, we must consider these leaves (at that time), as common and abundant <u>everywhere and anywhere in the Garden</u> of Eden. Giving us the assumption of being the most available material, to cover or to resolve an emergency in such circumstances.

Furthermore, the Bible does not describe the details; related to the quality and texture of such fig's leaves. It just presents the action taken immediately, in circumstances of desperation and the necessity to cover their nakedness in such a hurry. We can go on and on in the possibilities of interpretation about Adam and Eve's decision to choose these fig's leaves. A Topic that the bible does not give to many details about it. But the reality is that from this point on, they knew something was wrong; *"their eyes were opened to see and comprehend that they were naked"*. And this problem to bare such understanding or shame, was created by themselves. So, in the subconscious mind of culpability, they understood that they put themselves in this situation. And now, being aware of such failure or disobedience, they felt the desperate need to take action about this problem. And the most practical solution that came to their mind, was to make vestments with the fig's leaves.

Perhaps, in all the knowledge that they acquire eating the forbidden fruit, they did not conceive in their mind, that those leaves will not last very long. Or perhaps they knew that those fig's leaves will perish soon or later, but they just want to cover their naked body in this tragic emergency. And as we can read later in the scriptures, The Loving Father God came with a better solution to this problem, covering them with skin garments, that will last a little longer.

Summary & Reflections of this Topic

Having examined the profound symbolism of fig leaves, and the deliberate mystery surrounding the tree of such fruit, we now see how Genesis invites readers into a deeper reflection on human nature, obedience, and the universal experience of temptation. The fig leaf serves not just as a practical covering but as a powerful emblem of human fragility, and the limits of self-made solutions in confronting shame and guilt. With these insights, we can approach the unfolding biblical narrative—and our own lives—with renewed attention to the dynamics of faith, responsibility, and grace, recognizing that the story of Eden speaks across time to every person facing moments of decision and transformation.

Chapter 9:

Strange 'SKIN'! ...& (?)

What Animal? – Why Unidentified?

(GENESIS 3:21)

"The LORD God made garments of skin… and clothed them."

Coverings of Mystery: The Enigma of the <u>Non-Described Skin Garments</u>; Genesis 3:21

"The LORD God made <u>garments of skin</u> and clothed them." These few words from Genesis have puzzled readers for centuries, hiding a mystery that invites us to look deeper beyond the surface. **What exactly were these garments?** <u>Why did God provide them after the Fall</u>? Were they simply a **practical solution or something far more symbolic?** Beneath this brief sentence lies a story about identity, transformation, and the complex relationship between humanity and divinity. As we explore this passage, we will uncover how these early coverings speak to themes of vulnerability and grace, sacrifice and mercy—questions that continue to stir debate among theologians and scholars today. This moment reveals much about how ancient narratives shape our understanding of human nature, responsibility, and the search for meaning in both ancient times and modern faith.

Possibility of Interpretation 1:

Attempts to Interpreting the Garments:

Divine Provision or Sacrifice?

Genesis 3:21 marks a turning point in the biblical narrative: ***"And the LORD God made for Adam and for his wife garments of skins and clothed them."*** This terse verse, containing the earliest explicit mention of clothing after the Fall, has drawn centuries of attention for what it says, and perhaps even more for what it leaves unsaid. Within its brief wording lies a richness of ambiguity, inviting speculation and generating diverse interpretations across theological, historical, and cultural lines. It has become much more than a matter-of-fact description of new apparel; it is a passage laden with deep questions about vulnerability, shame, mercy, sacrifice, and the changing relationship between God and humanity.

And let us keep in mind, that **the Holy Scriptures <u>do not mention any animal's name.</u>** <u>Neither is mentioned the details of the process on how God obtained the skin garment</u>. It just remarks the intervention of our Lord God and <u>Loving Father, taking care of a crucial necessity</u> for his <u>beloved human creation</u>, in a condition and circumstance of unprotection. Therefore, **the type of animal the skin was taken from remain as a mystery.**

One influential interpretive tradition reads this moment as a profound act of divine mercy. According to this perspective, the making of garments signals God's gracious response to newly exposed frailty. Adam and Eve had sewn fig leaves to cover themselves when their eyes were opened to their nakedness, but God's clothing replaces their inadequate efforts with something more fitting. This is seen not as a punitive act, but as <u>a gesture of protection and compassionate provision</u> in a world now colored by threat and hardship Proponents of this view see God's hands not as those of a judge but of a caretaker, interested in restoring dignity and shielding His creations from further harm. Layers of biblical language reinforce this motif: the act of covering is frequently associated with God's grace, as seen in passages where He spreads His "wings" as a refuge, or when His attributes are described as a "shield." The lasting association of clothing, with covering shame and restoring honor is reflected elsewhere, such as when the loving father clothes the returning prodigal son, or when God commands garments for priests that cover nakedness — connecting the motif to identity, status, and belonging.

Possibility of Interpretation 2:

Favor, or Idea of Paying a Price

In contrast, a second influential interpretive strand sees in the garments of skin; the shadow of a first sacrifice. Here, the very material of the garments — animal skin (possibly) — suggests that a life was taken from another living entity, to deal with this human shame and guilt. This line of thought argues that the passage is more than a merciful covering; it is the inauguration of atonement through bloodshed. Adam and Eve's new clothing is not just practical protection but a symbol: even at this earliest moment, **the covering of their nakedness comes at a cost**. The shedding of blood is therefore seen as a prototype of the future sacrificial system that stretches across the Old Testament, from Abel's "more acceptable" offering to the animals slain on the Day of Atonement, and even into the Christian understanding of the **"Lamb of God"** as a final, perfect sacrifice. The connection is drawn between the initial garments and the later scriptural descriptions of sacrifice as both covering and cleansing — deepening the sense that something profound and costly lies beneath this ancient story.

The ambiguity of the passage — <u>no mention of an explicit sacrifice</u>, **no detail about the type of animal**, <u>no description of the process</u> — fuels ongoing debate. Was this 'simply an act of providence', or the dawn of a ritual that would define generations? Jewish and Christian traditions alike have created imaginative explanations to fill the silence. Some rabbinic sources maintain that humans were not originally covered in skin at all, but in brilliance or light, and that the loss of "garments of light" was part of the Fall's tragedy.

Another Possibility of Interpretation:

(Theological)

Transformation and Identity: The Lasting Impact of Covering Nakedness... and more than that.

After Adam and Eve leave Eden, the 'garments of skin' given to them become more than simple coverings. This act signals a transformation, highlighting how the fallout from their disobedience results in a new level of human awareness and responsibility. There is a noticeable movement from innocence toward self-consciousness and shame, as seen in their initial attempt to cover themselves with fig leaves. The divine provision of more durable garments underscores the seriousness of their new condition. No longer are Adam and Eve simply creatures in harmony with their surroundings; they are now beings who experience separation, vulnerability, and the burden of moral knowledge.

The change in how they see themselves emerges as one of the most powerful aspects of this moment. The act of wearing garments shifts human identity from <u>naked shamelessness</u> to a new understanding of the self one, that recognizes difference and the weight of personal responsibility. Relationships are affected as well. Adam and Eve's relationship with God is marked by distance and a need for mediation, while their relationship with each other is altered by new feelings of shame and mutual awareness. This change echoes in the developing norms and expectations about modesty, privacy, and the nature of social interactions. Clothing is not only a practical necessity but a social marker that defines status, belonging, and morality

Clothing immediately takes on symbolic meaning. The process by which the 'garments of skin' replace the hastily fashioned fig leaves, indicates an elevation of culture from makeshift solutions to deliberate action. In Genesis, this is the moment when humans first become creators in their own right, shaping materials to meet needs both physical and social. As societies develop, these foundational actions carry forward. Attire becomes a canvas for creative expression and a system for transmitting values. Modesty norms, for example, reflect evolving ideas about what should be hidden or revealed, and why these distinctions matter. The first garments shape communal expectations, enable distinctions between groups, and foster the development of social identities.

The symbolism of clothing in religious cultures expands dramatically in later biblical narratives. Wearing special garments marks transitions—priests, prophets, and even royalty don distinctive clothing for ritual purposes. These traditions find their roots in the initial act of God clothing humanity. Over time, both Jewish and early Christian communities use clothing as a metaphor for moral and spiritual transformation. Paul's exhortation to *"clothe yourself in Christ"* is an evolution of this theme, suggesting that what one wears expresses deeper truths about identity and virtue. This metaphor not only highlights personal transformation but also signals full membership within a community set apart by shared beliefs and ethical commitments.

Other Ideas & Possibilities of Interpretations:

Interpretations of this passage remain vibrant and <u>often sharply divided</u>. Some theologians read the garments as an expression of divine mercy alone, a moment of kindness in the midst of consequences. Others see layers of meaning—signals of death's entrance into the world, the emergence of rituals that involve animal sacrifice, and the institution of symbolic structures that teach about the costs and promises of restored relationship with the divine. This ongoing debate keeps Genesis 3:21 at the center of discussions about faith, identity, and the complex interplay between justice and mercy. The passage continues to offer fertile ground for discussions on human dignity, accountability, and the hope for transformation, resonating with readers who search for meaning in their own lives and communities.

Summary & Reflections of this Topic

Having explored the many layers of meaning behind the garments of skin in **Genesis 3:21**—from divine mercy to sacrificial symbolism and their profound impact on human identity—we can now approach this ancient text with a richer perspective that embraces its mystery and complexity. This passage invites us not only to reflect on humanity's transformed relationship with God but also to consider how themes of vulnerability, responsibility, and redemption continue to shape our understanding of faith and community today. As readers and seekers of truth, we are called to engage thoughtfully with these interpretations, recognizing that the story of the first clothing points toward a deeper hope: the possibility of restoration through grace, sacrifice, and ongoing transformation in our own lives and spiritual journeys.

Chapter 10:

Strange 'Sword'!

…Of What? For What? And Why?

(GENESIS 3: 24)

"So He drove out the man; and He placed at the east of the garden of Eden cherubim, and a <u>flaming</u> sword which <u>turned every way</u>, to keep the way of the tree of life."

José E. Espinoza

Sword of Flames: 'Barring the Way Back' to The Tree of Life

"The gate is closed forever," (or at least for this era) our ancestors, grandparents, or even our parents had once told us that. As one of my ancestors once told me that, with his voice heavy with a weight I did not yet understand. They spoke of a place lost—not just to time, but to something deeper, a boundary no one could cross on their own. That image stayed with me: a fierce guard standing watch, a barrier that marks more than exile or punishment. It is not simply about loss; it is about a line drawn between what was, and what can never be reclaimed without help from beyond our effort attempt. In this chapter, we explore the nature of that boundary, its guardians, and the mysterious forces that hold the way back—a story that invites us to rethink separation, protection, and the hope that lies beyond what seems forever barred.

Possibility of Interpretation 1:

The <u>Flaming Sword</u>: Symbolism, Protection, and Divine Boundaries

The flaming sword at Eden's entrance in **Genesis 3:24** provides a vivid symbol of divine enforcement, boundary, and loss. With Adam and Eve's expulsion from the garden, God does not merely close the gates. He establishes an unmistakable barrier, placing cherubim and a **<u>sword blazing with fire</u> that <u>turns in every direction</u>.** This sword operates as an extension of God's authority, visibly marking the transition from innocence to estrangement for humanity. Its presence transforms Eden's edge into an inviolable point of separation, emphasizing both judgment and protection. The text underscores that this boundary was not arbitrary but a purposeful establishment by the Creator: *"He drove out the man; and he placed at the east of the garden of Eden cherubim, and a flaming <u>sword</u> which <u>turned every way</u>, to keep the way of the tree of life"*.

In its fierce motion, the sword upholds the seriousness of the divine verdict. It does not remain still, nor is it a passive warning. Its ceaseless, ever-turning blaze communicates that the path to Eden remains closed—not just for Adam and Eve but for all who follow. There is no period in which the sword becomes silent or retracts; it is a constant, kinetic force, signaling that access to the garden's heart is not subject to human negotiation. The whirling nature of the sword serves as a persistent testimony to the reality of exclusion. Eden's peace and communion with God now exist beyond reach (in this era), a symbol that innocence, once surrendered, cannot be retrieved through effort, force, or intuition. The blocked way stands as undeniable evidence of what has been lost and cannot be recovered by will or longing alone. This aligns with how the consequences of the fall extend beyond mere punishment, forging a perpetual reminder of the separation brought by disobedience

The sword's stationing before the tree of life brings focus to another important function: **preventing Adam and Eve from accessing immortality in their fallen state**. The concern is not only with physical removal from the garden, but with a deeper existential prohibiting. As God notes, in **Genesis 3:22** Saying; *"lest he put forth his hand, <u>and take also of the tree of life</u>, and eat, <u>and live forever</u>."* The sword, burning and unapproachable, ensures that humanity cannot perpetuate their condition of separation and rebellion. This blocking points to the gravity of the rupture—a world marked by broken fellowship, pain, and death—where living forever would cement corruption in the individual and in creation. The very presence of the sword reveals that restoration to eternal life must come by means other than self-initiative; redemption is a necessary act of divine grace, not a result of human striving or encroachment.

Possibility of Interpretation 2:

Visualization and Idea of the Sword

The appearance of the flaming sword also evokes a compelling sense of awe and holy fear. While fear can be understood as punitive, it also promotes reverence and respect for the divine presence. In biblical expression, **fire signifies God's radiance, power, and separateness**. The sword's incessant blaze both deters and teaches, warning humans against presumption while inviting them to ponder the sanctity of what they have lost. This combination of warning and awe mirrors the scenes in later Scripture, such as the fire and cloud on Mount Sinai or the burning bush before Moses, where God's holiness is accentuated with perilous beauty. The sword, through its flame, becomes a lesson—not just in punishment but in the right ordering of life in relation to the divine.

Through all these perspectives, the flaming sword embodies the themes of divine judgment, vigilant protection, the irreversibility of innocence lost, and the preservation of the divine order. It serves as a sign that Eden, with its unhindered relationship between creation and Creator, belongs to another time and condition. The imagery teaches that God both guards and grieves the boundary, holding both justice and mercy in balance. This entrance, once free and open, now serves as a reminder of what true holiness and fellowship require, encouraging humility in the face of the divine. In contemplating the sword, readers come to understand the depth of the division between humanity and God, and how restoration cannot be claimed but must be given, pointing forward to the hope of redemption beyond the sword's reach.

<u>Cherubim</u>: Guardianship, Holiness, and Restoration Through Grace

Possibilities of Interpretation about <u>Cherubim</u>:

Cherubim occupy a place of highest distinction among the spiritual hosts in the biblical tradition. From the moment God places them at the entrance of Eden with a flaming sword, they step forth not only as sentinels, but also as exalted figures set apart for **guarding** the sacred **mysteries of God's presence**. Their role as the first line of <u>protection</u> after humanity's transgression marks a dramatic shift from harmony toward separation; they stand as both **protectors of holiness** and, paradoxically, witnesses to humanity's loss of direct access to divine fellowship.

Scripture repeatedly attributes remarkable authority and glory to the cherubim. Exodus links them directly with God's dwelling, for it is between the cherubim on the mercy seat of the Ark of the Covenant that God promises to meet with Moses. According to **Exodus 25:22**. These angelic beings are not mere decoration. Their images dominate the sanctuary: *"two cherubim of gold"* crafted to stretch their wings over the ark—faces turned toward each other, looking toward the mercy seat, their posture capturing a sense of awe and vigilance. As later generations enter Solomon's Temple, they again encounter immense cherubim carved from wood and overlaid with gold, their wings spanning the entire width of the Holy of Holies. (**1 Kings 6:23-28**). The sacred space becomes an echo of Eden, with cherubim forming living boundaries separating God's immediate presence from those who are unworthy or unclean.

Ezekiel's visions further amplify the cherubim's grandeur. When he describes his encounter with the living creatures beneath God's throne, the cherubim appear both **awe-inspiring and mysterious**. These beings possess four faces—of a **human, a lion, an ox, and an eagle**—suggesting wisdom, strength, service, and majesty. Their multiple wings and their shining, fiery appearance recall the sword of flames at Eden's gate. The fusion of these characteristics points to their supernatural authority and sets them apart from other spiritual figures.

Throughout the Old Testament, the appearance of cherubim always marks a boundary: the division between holy and profane, the heavenly and the earthly, the sacred and the common. Their presence in the tabernacle veil—embroidered and woven into the very texture of the boundary that separated the Holy Place from the Most Holy Place—underscores the seriousness of approaching God. As the veil hangs, it silently preaches the message of restricted access and the impossibility of casually entering divine presence. The cherubim woven there serve as continual reminders of the flaming sword that safeguarded Eden, signifying that any attempt to cross without atonement or invitation risks judgment. In this light, the cherubim must be understood not as capricious guards but as symbols of both God's mercy and His unapproachable holiness.

This symbolism deepens when considering their placement in Israel's worship. **Psalms 99:1** proclaims, *"The Lord reigns, let the nations tremble; He sits enthroned between the cherubim."* The image here is one of majestic authority and overwhelming holiness. To "dwell between the cherubim" is to occupy the very center of the sacred, a position safeguarded with a seriousness intensified by the events of the fall. In **Hebrews 9:5**, the cherubim atop the mercy seat are described as "cherubim of glory," the site on which the visible presence of God rested. Their wings, stretched protectively over the atonement cover, speak both of guardianship and invitation—access, but only by the path of sacrifice.

As the narrative unfolds, the continued prominence of the cherubim hints at God's enduring desire for restoration. **Their stationed watch does not close Eden's gate forever**; instead, it preserves the way until reconciliation becomes possible. **The flaming sword flashes** not only as a warning but as a signpost, pointing to the sacrificial path required for renewed communion. Eventually, the tearing of the temple veil at Christ's sacrifice replaces the guarded barrier with direct access, signaling that, though humanity cannot reopen Eden by effort, God Himself will restore the way by grace.

In every appearance, the cherubim reveal the weight of lost innocence and the steadfast hope for restoration. Their role both restricts and anticipates—underscoring that spiritual intimacy can be regained only on God's terms, by His initiatory grace, never by human striving alone. This pattern anchors the biblical promise of redemption, in which boundaries once imposed by sin become thresholds of hope. **The cherubim remain at the threshold**, reminders both of separation and the divine longing to dwell once again with humanity.

Summary & Reflections of this Chapter

Having explored the profound symbolism of the flaming sword and cherubim at Eden's entrance, we now understand these figures as more than mere biblical curiosities; they embody the deep spiritual realities of judgment, protection, and separation that followed humanity's fall. Their presence teaches us about God's holiness and the serious boundaries established between Creator and creation, while also pointing forward to the hope of restoration—a restoration made possible only through divine grace. With this insight, readers and scholars alike can approach Scripture with a renewed appreciation for how these ancient symbols shape our understanding of sin, mercy, and redemption, encouraging thoughtful reflection on the ways God continues to guard and prepare the path toward reconciliation.

Chapter 11:

Mysterious 'TREE #2'

Which one? What for? & Where is it?

(GENESIS 3:22) *"...and take also from the tree of life, and..."*

(GENESIS 3:24) *"...to guard the way to the tree of life."*

(Tree of Life Restricted/Protected)

Mysterious <u>Tree of Life</u>: Forbidden Forever?

What lies behind the guarded entrance to the <u>Tree of Life</u>? Why did God decide to close off access to something that seems to promise eternal life? And what does this restriction mean for humanity's place in the world, both in ancient times and today? For centuries, readers and scholars alike have wrestled with these questions, seeking to understand the deeper reasons woven into the story of Eden. The loss of the Tree is not simply about punishment or denial—it touches on complex themes of mercy, prevention, and hope that challenge our understanding of divine intention. At the same time, the persistent human desire to reach beyond mortality, reflected in countless stories and beliefs across cultures, points to a profound longing that has shaped spiritual thought throughout history. This chapter invites you to explore these questions anew, uncovering insights that reveal why the Tree's forbidden nature holds meaning far beyond its immediate context, and how it continues to inspire hopes for restoration and healing.

Possibility of Interpretation 1:

Divine Motives Behind <u>Restricted Access</u> to <u>the Tree of Life</u>

Exploring the theological and scriptural implications, of why <u>God restricted access to the Tree of Life</u> in **Genesis 3:22-24,** reveals a purposeful pattern woven into the early biblical narrative. God's decision to set boundaries after humanity's transgression reaches beyond mere punishment. <u>These verses signal a deep concern for the human condition in its fallen state</u>, inviting adults, biblical scholars, theology students, religious educators, and lay readers to understand **God's motives** as layered and ultimately merciful.

Prevention of Eternal Fallenness

Genesis 3:22-24 shows a striking interplay between divine knowledge and vulnerable humanity: ***"And the LORD God said, 'The man has now become like one of us, knowing good and evil. He must not be allowed to reach out his hand and take also from <u>the tree of life</u> and <u>eat, and live forever.</u>' So the LORD God banished him from the Garden of Eden..."*** The narrative presents a scenario where permitting immediate continued access to the Tree of Life, would have fixed humanity in a permanent state of spiritual and physical corruption. In other words, once sin had entered, allowing endless existence would mean that decay, disorder, and alienation (or disconnection) from God could never be reversed. '<u>Mortality;</u>, therefore, becomes a '**<u>temporary hopeful boundary</u>'**—a chance for the story to change, <u>for redemption to occur</u>. The seriousness of the fall is underscored here; the implications of sin extend beyond personal disobedience, to shape the very parameters of human existence. This restriction is not solely punitive, but a way of <u>preventing the tragedy of eternal separation</u>, a measure **protecting humanity from the irreversible consequences of corrupted immortality**. In this way, <u>mortality can be read as a gift that holds open the possibility of change</u>, growth, and restoration.

Mercy (Hidden) in Exclusion

Examining the expulsion from Eden in this light reveals an unexpected dimension of mercy. God's removal of access to the Tree of Life does not merely impose punishment; it draws a protective border. By keeping humanity from sealing its corrupted fate, God demonstrates a form of care—shielding people from what would otherwise be an unending experience of suffering and alienation. The closed gate and the flaming sword at Eden's eastern boundary become vivid images not only of judgment but of divine compassion in action **(Genesis 3:24).** They serve as reminders that boundaries can exist for the sake of well-being, with human suffering limited and hope preserved for something better. This banishment, reframed, reveals God's patience and reluctance to allow permanent harm, creating conditions where healing and reconciliation remain possible. Rather than being arbitrary or cruel, the exclusion incorporates a logic aimed at future good, setting limits on despair so hope can survive.

Hope Postponed

By forbidding access to the Tree of Life, the narrative keeps alive a vision of ultimate restoration. The Tree remains, guarded and unreachable, a symbol not of lost privilege but of deferred possibility. In Genesis, the tree's continued existence preserves the hope that paradise, though lost, is not destroyed forever. This theme persists through scripture, where Edenic imagery and the quest for lost intimacy with God reappear. The Tree of Life's restriction thus maintains anticipation, for a day when relationship and immortality might be restored. Deferred hope becomes an animating force, sustaining the human longing for reunion with the divine. Biblical echoes of the Tree of Life throughout later texts, from glimpses in the Psalms and Proverbs to prophetic visions, reinforce its enduring importance, encouraging faithfulness and expectation that the blessings of Eden are not gone, only waiting their appointed time.

Redemptive Shadows

The story of the Tree of Life casts long shadows across scripture, returning at key moments to signify God's redemptive intentions. Proverbs describes wisdom as *"a tree of life to those who take hold of her"* **(Proverbs 3:18),** connecting the tree of life's fruit to the pursuit of virtue and healing. <u>Revelation's final vision restores access to this tree of life</u>, showing it at the center of **<u>the renewed creation</u>**: The final book of the bible (ending of the 'New testament'), called 'Revelation or Apocalypses', at the last chapter of the Scriptures states; *"On either side of the river stood the tree of life, bearing twelve crops of fruit… and the leaves of the tree are for the healing of the nations."* **(Revelation 22:2)**. These echoes reveal that God's decision at Eden was not a final rejection, but the start of a longer journey toward reconciliation and renewal. The recurring symbol of the Tree assures readers that the promise withheld at the beginning will be fulfilled at the end, and that God's purposes are always oriented toward restoration and belonging.

Desire for access to the Tree of Life lingers in the human spirit, its meaning expanding through law, wisdom, and prophecy. This longing for immortality and restoration carries forward, shaping myths and spiritual yearning across cultures. The Genesis account thus plants seeds for understanding both the cost and promise of what it means to be fully human in relation to God, infusing history with a hope left waiting at Eden's gate—always beckoning from beyond the boundaries.

Possibility of Interpretation 2:

Humanity's Longing for Immortality Through the Tree of Life

Longing for the Tree of Life shapes the imagination of civilizations and underlies the essence of countless myths, scriptures, and philosophical systems. The Tree of Life's withdrawal in Genesis is not only a lost paradise but a wound on the collective human psyche, becoming an archetype around which cultures build their deepest stories of hope and restoration. People over centuries, sensing a fracture from primordial wholeness, return to tales of a sacred center, often embodied in trees or lush gardens. The roots of these stories run deep, suggesting the human soul always hungers for a source of healing, immortality, and spiritual reunion.

Ancient Mesopotamian myths tell of a cosmic tree in the center of the world, stretching between earth and heaven as the pillar of creation. The Assyrian sacred tree stands as a symbol of divine favor and the ruler's right to govern, echoing the idea of divine gifts being mediated by a tree-like axis. In Norse myth, Yggdrasil, the immense ash tree, connects all realms, its branches and roots nourishing gods and mortals alike, offering both wisdom and the possibility of renewal after cosmic destruction. In the Hindu tradition, the Ashvattha, or World Tree, represents eternal life, its roots in the divine, its branches touching mortal experience. These myths reflect a lingering memory of unity and wholeness, with the Tree acting as a sacred signpost pointing toward lost harmony.

Scriptural traditions embed the longing for restoration within foundational stories. In **Genesis 3**, humanity's exile from Eden and the Tree of Life signals more than lost immortality; it inaugurates a sacred hope. Cherubim guard the Tree ***"lest he reach out his hand… and eat, and live forever"*** (**Genesis 3:22-24**), framing divine restriction as mercy, sparing humanity from unending separation. Eschatological visions renew the promise: Revelation describes the Tree of Life in the New Jerusalem, whose leaves are ***"for the healing of the nations"*** (**Revelation 22:2**), anchoring hope in eventual restoration, healing, and reunion with the divine.

Spiritual seekers and mystics advance a similar yearning—the pursuit of transformative knowledge or immortality. In Jewish Kabbalah, the Tree of Life appears as the diagram of sefirot, signifying the journey of the soul back to its source.

Heroic quest narratives across world literature reinforce the role of the lost or hidden tree as the object of pursuit. In the epic of Gilgamesh, the search for the plant of immortality mirrors the yearning to reverse mortality. In Arthurian legend, the quest for the Holy Grail often unfolds in enchanted groves or alongside sacred trees, signifying the restoration of grace. Even the biblical narrative of exile and return is taken up in journey tales, from Moses' vision of the burning bush—a fiery emblem of presence and provision—to Christ's passion in a garden, framing the restoration arc in vegetal imagery. Each story offers more than adventure: the quest for the Tree is a journey toward renewal, resilience, and redemption.

The memory of Eden serves as an undercurrent of spiritual and ethical thought, exerting force upon moral aspiration. The notion that exile awakens longing for divine proximity, shapes the formation of conscience and guides the pursuit of virtue. In rabbinic literature, the gates of Eden open each Sabbath, suggesting that moments of wholeness remain accessible through spiritual practice. The motif of returning to an original blessing inspires practices of compassion, justice, and unity, grounding ethical visions in the hope for ultimate restoration. The persistent call of the Tree of Life, then, nurtures both the imagination and the will, guiding humanity toward hope through the shadows of exile and longing

Summary and Reflections of This Topic

Understanding the divine reasons behind restricting access to the Tree of Life opens a window into God's mercy, protection, and enduring hope for humanity. Recognizing that this limitation preserves the possibility of redemption, rather than final rejection allows us to see mortality not as a curse but as a necessary step toward healing and restoration. The persistent human yearning for the Tree, echoed across myths, scripture, and spiritual traditions, reminds us that the story is far from over. With this insight, readers and scholars alike can approach Genesis with renewed appreciation for its depth and complexity, inspiring further exploration of how these ancient themes continue to shape faith, ethics, and the longing for ultimate reunion with the divine.

Chapter 12:

Strange 'Sign on Cain'!

What was it? & Why?

(GENESIS 4:15) *"…Whoever kills Cain, vengeance shall be taken on him sevenfold."* … *The Lord Put a 'Sign/(Mark)' On Cain so …"*

Rare 'SIGN' on Cain: ('Mysterious MARK')

José E. Espinoza

Strange 'SIGN' on Cain

"...Whoever kills Cain, vengeance shall be taken on him sevenfold." *... The Lord Put a 'Sign/(Mark)' On Cain so ..."* (Genesis 4:15.)

These words introduce a paradox that has confounded readers for centuries—**a mark** both **mysterious** and meaningful, bearing the weight of protection and punishment at the same time. The brief mention in Genesis invites questions rather than answers: **What exactly is this mark?** Why does it shield a murderer from harm while condemning him to exile? Was this a visible sign worn on the skin, or something unseen that marks his very being? This enigmatic detail opens a door to explore how ancient texts wrestle with justice, mercy, and the complexity of divine judgment. As we engage with this rare biblical symbol, we discover a story that speaks beyond its immediate narrative, challenging assumptions about sin, punishment, and the fragile balance between isolation and survival. The mark's silence and ambiguity prompt us to look deeper into the tensions it carries—between wrath and restraint, alienation and care—and to consider how its legacy echoes through generations, shaping ideas about human nature and divine grace.

Possibility of Interpretation 1:

Attempts to interpret The <u>Unknown</u> Mark's <u>Identity</u>: Ambiguity, Purpose, and Symbolism

In **Genesis 4:15**, the arrival of the mark on Cain transforms a personal transgression into a multi-layered mystery, where divine retribution bends into something more complicated than vengeance. The narrative flows from an act of murder to a sentence that is as much about protection as it is punishment. Cain, condemned to a fate as a restless wanderer, voices a desperate fear: whoever finds him will kill him for his crime. The reply is **the mark—enigmatic**, unelaborated, yet potent. God's gesture ensures that anyone who kills Cain will suffer vengeance sevenfold, but this protection also comes with a forced separation. Cain is shielded, yet cut adrift. The wilderness becomes his only home, even as his life is kept from those who might exact familial or communal justice. The duality creates a lasting paradox. The mark repels, yet preserves; it forbids vengeance while upholding the certainty of Cain's solitary existence. In protecting Cain, God upends both conventional justice and unmitigated wrath, sketching a divine character marked by restraint as much as by holy intimidation.

José E. Espinoza

Protection and separation intertwine in the way the text presents the consequences. Cain's safety is guaranteed, but the cost is exile. Scriptural language according to **Genesis 4:14**, makes plain that Cain becomes *"a fugitive and a wanderer on the earth,"* set apart from settled society—a kind of living symbol of divine warning and mercy combined. This split experience recurs elsewhere in biblical literature, where God's intervention can intentionally complicate human responses to sin: mercy tempers judgment, grace mingles with consequence. In Cain's story, protection is inseparable from alienation, and the mark stands as the visible or invisible boundary between acceptance and perpetual wandering.

What the mark actually is has fueled centuries of debate. Some traditions see it as a tangible change, something seen by others—perhaps a blemish or a brand that warns would-be assailants, perhaps even a dramatic physical alteration. The drive to read the mark as visible finds some purchase in the narrative itself, where fear of random retribution prompts Cain's plea and God's answer, implying a mark that others recognize. On this view, the mark is a safeguard, operating in the visible realm, deploying God's promise as a deterrent woven into Cain's own flesh.

Possibility of Interpretation 2:

(Traditional & Theological Ideas)

Symbolic and Spiritual Remark

Others argue the mark is spiritual—an internal <u>**sign,**</u> legible chiefly to God, or perhaps to those attuned to divine communication. The ambiguity in the text supports this reading: Genesis never specifies any physical transformation, leaving the reader with a token of divine promise—the Hebrew word "oth"—whose substance could be visible, symbolic, or entirely spiritual. This interpretive openness has fascinated Jewish and Christian commentators. Some rabbinic voices propose supernatural symbols. Late medieval artists have sometimes rendered Cain with horns, a sign of misapprehended tradition, while others depict him unmarked, haunted merely by guilt or spiritual loss. The spiritual reading finds resonance in the way biblical marks, often exist as covenantal signs—like the rainbow of Noah or the circumcision given to Abraham's descendants—visible to some, but laden with spiritual meaning.

This ambiguity deepens upon exploring the Hebrew term **"oth,"** translated in **Genesis 4:15** as **"mark."** The word's semantic range encompasses ***sign,*** pledge, and token, each with layers of meaning that shift with context and translation. Outside **Genesis 4:15**, "oth" usually connotes <u>symbolic or protective signs</u> rather than punitive brands. Some English Bibles have preferred ***"sign"*** or <u>"token"</u> over ~~"mark"~~ in recent translations, downplaying physical connotation in favor of a broader or more abstract indication of divine action. This subtle variation in language has significant impacts on how readers imagine the event. By making the term slippery—sometimes physical, sometimes figurative—the text both engages and frustrates the search for certainty. Interpretation is shaped as much by translation as by theological bias and cultural context.

The mark's legacy outlives Cain. Across history, it has gathered meanings that reach far beyond Genesis. Medieval and early modern Christian communities sometimes misapplied it to justify prejudices, associating the mark with visible, racialized difference—a distortion rejected by contemporary scholarship and modern religious leaders. Artists and authors have seized on the motif to explore outsider status, justice, or mercy: the mark becomes a badge, a stigma, or a secret grace. In theology, it serves as a shorthand for the complex interplay between the desire for order and the need for compassion, for punishment that breaks boundaries yet refuses to annihilate. The very uncertainty of the mark—its quietly shifting shape, its layered meanings, the tension between protection and exile—has ensured its endurance as a symbol that eludes a single interpretation. The mark keeps the reader lingering at the crossroads of divine justice and mercy, always asking what it means to be set apart, protected, and yet fundamentally alone.

José E. Espinoza

One more Possibility of Interpretation:

(Theological)

Aftermath: <u>Cain's Legacy</u> and the Shaping of <u>Humanity's Fate</u>

After the mysterious mark is set upon Cain, it does far more than resolve an immediate crisis. It establishes a pattern of living with consequences, where justice is tempered with a peculiar mercy. The mark, acting as both warning and safeguard, becomes a catalyst. Cain is banished from God's presence, condemned to restlessness, and distanced from the earth, yet his very survival is protected by the mark—a visible restraint placed upon the urge for retribution among others. This mingling of judgment and preservation distinguishes his fate and ripples into the narratives of exile, kinship, and communal boundaries in later biblical history.

The mark's first and most visible effect is to inaugurate exile as a consequence for grave wrongdoing. When Cain laments, *"You have driven me this day from the ground; and from Your face I shall be hidden. I shall be a fugitive and a vagabond on the earth, and it will happen that anyone who finds me will kill me,"* the response is not simple abandonment but the imposition of the mark to prevent summary vengeance **(Genesis 4:14, NKJV)** Cain's exile is the original pattern, tracing a path lived by later figures, whose banishment echoes Cain's predicament. The experience of separation is thus not merely external but spiritual, as the stories caution against assuming that outward prosperity or continued existence alone signals divine approval.

Yet, Cain's restlessness serves as fertile ground for the next significant development—the creation of human society. Genesis reveals that in his exile, **Cain...** ***"built a city, and <u>called</u> the name of the city after the name of his son—<u>Enoch</u>"***. **(Genesis 4:17, NKJV).** What at first seems a contradiction—founding civilization while cursed to wander—actually spotlights a paradoxical legacy. The descendants of Cain, known for ingenuity and the forging of new beginnings, chart out an inheritance of craft, adaptation, and even cultural advancement. Still, their story is shaded by the original violence; Lamech, a later descendent, boasts of a vengeance seventy-seven times greater than Cain's, twisting the principle of divine restraint into personal escalation. This tension becomes foundational. The city, product of the marked one's line, stands both as testimony to human creativity and a signpost for the dangers of progress unmoored from moral constraint. In biblical perspective, the city of Cain foreshadows future societies where the potential for justice and for corruption grows in equal measure.

The introduction of the mark also sets a powerful precedent for the boundaries of human justice. Within ancient societies, the threat of endless cycles of revenge was potent; the blood feud could easily spiral beyond control. The mark interrupts this trajectory. God's word was clear: *"whoever kills Cain, vengeance shall be taken on him sevenfold"*. (**Genesis 4:15, NKJV**). Divine law invokes a limit, establishing that justice must not devolve into unchecked retaliation. This motif recurs in laws that follow, including the *<u>lex talionis</u>—"*<u>an eye for an eye</u>"—which, contrary to assumptions of harshness, actually restricts vengeance by imposing measure and proportion. Cain's mark can thus be seen as the root of divine mercy intervening in human affairs, curbing excessive violence and urging for social restraint.

José E. Espinoza

Generational Echoes and Evolving Responsibility

As generations pass, the significance of the mark and its complex message persist in new forms. The account of Lamech vividly illustrates this. Unlike Cain, whose violence is met with divine protection, Lamech magnifies wrongdoing and vengeance through prideful assertion to his wives: *"If Cain is avenged sevenfold, then Lamech seventy-sevenfold"*. (**Genesis 4:24, NKJV.**) The escalation dramatizes the need for even firmer boundaries but simultaneously hints at the dangers of inherited guilt and the deepening of violence through lineage. **Meanwhile, the family tree of Adam and Eve divides**; from Cain, a tradition of wandering, creativity, and turmoil unfolds; from Seth, the "seed of the woman," emerges an alternate legacy rooted in grace and the quest for reconciliation with God.

Throughout, the theme of accountability—personal and communal—takes shape. Cain's mark reminds each generation that actions echo outward. The mark safeguards but does not erase consequences, a lesson later reinforced as descendants struggle with the same impulses for rebellion, exile, and the longing for belonging. This pattern shapes future biblical accounts, where separation and restoration, justice and mercy, continually reappear. In this way, the mark of Cain opens an ongoing dialogue about the meaning of responsibility, the reach of justice, and the enduring possibility of redemption. Every generation bearing its own marks must navigate the tension between the limits set by God and the call to live rightly within them.

Summary and Reflections of this Topic

Now that we have examined the mysterious mark or sign on Cain and its layered meanings of protection, punishment, exile, and mercy, we can better appreciate how this ancient symbol shapes our understanding of divine justice and human responsibility. The mark reminds us that judgment is not always straightforward; it balances restraint with consequence and sets a pattern for how people live with wrongdoing and grace. This story invites readers and scholars alike to explore the ongoing tension between separation and belonging, justice and compassion, and the ways these themes echo throughout biblical history and into our own lives. By engaging deeply with the mark's ambiguity and its lasting legacy, we open new paths for interpretation and teaching, enriching our grasp of Scripture and the complex nature of God's involvement in human affairs.

Chapter 13:

Rare Mention of; '3 Female Names Only!' ('Besides Eve') ...

Whom? Why? What About the Rest?

(GENESIS 4:19-22) <u>Women Names Mentioned</u> (Before the Flood) <u>Besides Eve;</u> "Adah", "Zillah", & "Naamah"

2 Wives; <u>Adah & Zillah</u>, 1 Sister; <u>Naamah</u>:

The Silenced Women Before the Flood

Why do some women in the earliest biblical stories have names while so many others remain unnamed and unseen? What does it mean when a text that carefully traces family lines chooses to highlight only a few female figures, and why are those choices important for how we understand history, memory, and faith? How can brief mentions in ancient scripture carry meanings that ripple through centuries of interpretation and belief? This chapter invites readers to consider these questions by focusing on **3 women;** *two wives* and *one sister* (<u>before the flood</u>), whose names appear in a time and place where silence about female identity was the norm. By examining their unique presence, we begin to uncover hidden layers in the narratives we often take for granted—layers that challenge us to think about; who is remembered, who is forgotten, and what impact these decisions have on our understanding of gender, authority, and tradition.

Possibility of Interpretation 1:

The Mystery and Implications of <u>Naming</u> Adah, Zillah, and Naamah

"Lamech took to himself two <u>wives</u>: the name of the one was <u>Adah</u>, and the name of the other, <u>Zillah.</u>" **(Genesis 4:19).** This short line in Genesis instantly makes Adah and Zillah stand out against the background of early biblical genealogies, **(before the flood)** <u>where almost every other woman remains unnamed</u>. Then few lines after on **Genesis 4:22** states; *"...and the sister of Tubal-cain was <u>Naamah.</u>"* And those are <u>the only 3 female names mentioned,</u> besides (the first wife and Matriarch) who was Eve. And so far, that is all we can find on the written records from **Genesis 1:1** up to **Genesis 7:12-13**. When *"The rain fell upon the earth..."*. <u>No other women's name is mentioned before the flood</u>. Their names echo in a male-dominated document that usually traces families from father to son. The sudden clarity of their presence, given the silence surrounding other women, transforms their mention into a mystery and a signal: something unusual is happening in the narrative that urges readers to look more closely.

Adah and Zillah's appearance is brief, but it carries weight. Lamech's declaration to them in **Genesis 4:23** occurs in a context charged with fresh violence and domination. The speech itself, a boastful verse of vengeance, addresses his wives by name. In a text where women are often described only as "wives" or "mothers". "sisters" or "daughters", without individual identity; this direct address elevates Adah and Zillah and places them at the center of a defining moment. In contrast, throughout pre-Flood genealogies like those of **Genesis 5**, the names of men are meticulously recorded while their wives, mothers, and daughters disappear from the written record. Even the name of **Naamah** is mentioned in a short sentence, as the ***sister of Tubal-cain***. This narrative habit not only marginalizes female figures but also frames history itself as; a mostly male affair.

Scholars have tried to explain why these women are missing. The first major explanation sees the omission as part of a 'Silent Majority.' Ancient storytelling often reflects the cultures in which <u>male achievements and lineages were preserved and celebrated</u>, while women's lives became invisible. Naming was a form of social power; <u>those who were named were remembered</u>, while those who were not faded into anonymity. This selective recording carried deep consequences, forging a template where men's stories appeared central by default. The erasure or omission of most women's names in genealogies may not have been accidental but operated as a deliberate choice rooted in patriarchal worldviews, ensuring that women's complex roles, experiences, and contributions were consistently overshadowed or lost. Several studies point out that many women's stories likely endured in oral tradition, handed down in families but denied a place in the scriptural record, which contributed to shaping centuries of gender norms and expectations.

The alternative explanation suggests that when Genesis names **<u>Adah</u> <u>and Zillah</u>**, it signals the emergence of something extraordinary. <u>Their naming disrupts male-centered storytelling</u>, suggesting they had roles or stories that stood out starkly enough to demand recording. <u>Some propose that the text calls attention to these women because they mark a turning point</u>—**the beginning of polygamy or the turning point of a particular lineage**. And at the same time we could; say <u>new domestic arrangements</u>, and <u>interlinked forms of power and violence</u>. Naming them may underline the seriousness or novelty of this development and invite readers to consider its ethical and theological consequences. It also establishes that, even in stories designed around men, women may shape events in ways <u>too significant to ignore</u>. The act of naming itself can be read as a subtle critique or challenge to patriarchal assumptions.

Examining other genealogical passages in Genesis, such as the line descents from Adam through Seth or from Noah and his sons, further highlights the pattern of neglect. Mothers, wives, and daughters are rarely named; when they are, as in the case of Sarah later in the Abrahamic narrative, it signals particular importance. For ancient communities, such patterns reflect more than editorial oversight—they reveal attitudes about who was deemed worthy of remembrance and what counted as historical achievement. Some modern commentators argue that consistent silence about most women's identities speaks to cultural and religious priorities, not mere accident. What gets written shapes not only memory but also power, as scripture became the root of generations of belief and practice.

The fact that <u>Adah and Zillah</u> emerge with names amid this silence has become a focal point for contemporary <u>theological debates</u>. Feminist theologians, for example, revisit their brief mention to interrogate the workings of memory, silence, and authority within scripture. <u>By spotlighting</u> **Adah and Zillah** <u>briefly as wives and matriarchs,</u> these scholars expose how sacred texts participated in both the erasure and selective recovery of women's stories. Their names have inspired some faith communities to grapple with questions about women's roles in leadership and interpretation, sometimes using their example to challenge exclusionary traditions or to imagine ways of reading scripture that are more inclusive, honest, and attentive to silences.

By giving names to these women and letting them stand at a crucial turning point, Genesis opens space for reflection on what it means to be remembered or forgotten, and who gets to tell the stories that define a people. The act of naming, like the act of omission, radiates consequences into later history—shaping the way gender, memory, and authority are understood. Besides the reality that **Naamah** is mentioned just once <u>as a sister</u>, the narrative power of **Adah and Zillah**'s story extends beyond its few lines, prompting new generations to reconsider who counts as worthy of remembrance and how sacred texts shape that judgment. Their mention gestures toward wider questions about legacy, lost voices, and the continuing meanings that grow from small details embedded in scripture.

Possibility of Interpretation 2:

Legacy, Symbolism, and Ongoing Controversy Surrounding Adah, Zillah, Naamah and the Unnamed Women

The brief record of Adah, Zillah and Naamah besides Eve, in the early chapters of Genesis (before the flood), punctuates a text otherwise dominated by unnamed women, setting them apart as unique markers in the genealogy of early humanity. Their presence, though confined to a handful of verses, confronts the reader with a paradox: **visibility within invisibility**. Named yet not elaborated on, Adah and Zillah signal not only the exceptionality of their mention, but also the systemic marginalization of women as active participants, and memory bearers in sacred history. This theme extends from earlier discussions on how rare female names highlight gendered silence. With so little disclosed, their narrative becomes emblematic of countless forgotten voices whose lived experiences, wisdom, and pain shaped the world of scripture but never reached the page.

Adah, Zillah, & Naamah as Vessels of Forgotten Stories

Scholars often interpret Adah, Zillah and Naamah as narrative signposts—symbols standing where narrative knowledge falls short. Theologians search for extra meaning behind the selection of their names, wondering if their rarity reflects a once-larger set of stories pruned by the theological priorities of the text. Rabbinic commentators sometimes expand on their brief mentions, placing them into **imagined scenarios** to address unanswered questions about lineage, family structures, or the spiritual dynamics of early society. In this framework, Adah, Zillah and Naamah become **reference points for persistent biblical mysteries**: genealogies with broken links, disappearances of female agency, and hints of trauma that the text narrates only by absence.

These gaps invite both scholarly humility and **creative possibility of interpretation.** Commentators grapple with the fact that **Adah and Zillah appear as silent companions** to Lamech, fathers of subsequent generations but with no recorded speech, actions, or reactions. And in the same manner, **the record of Naamah; just remain as a sister** of Tubal-cain. Some traditions weave possible motivations or fates for them, hypothesizing a role in the early spread of culture or hardship under patriarchal structures. Others use their silence to dwell on wider patterns of exclusion. Their story is less about their personal agency in the narrative, and more about how sacred history repeatedly denies women sustained presence and memory.

The Power and Burden of Biblical Omission

For many, the omission of detail is not a neutral oversight but a reflection of deep-seated social and theological hierarchies. Debates about the authority and value of women in ancient communities often circle around names like Adah, Zillah and Naamah, whose recorded existence both challenges and reaffirms the invisibility of others. They serve as case studies for examining how communal memory forms, emphasizing who gets remembered and why. In some rabbinic literature, their lack of substantive narrative opens the door for larger arguments about spiritual justice—the right to be seen and recognized in the collective story of God's people. Theirs is a legacy shaped by what is not said as much as by what is.

Explorations into their narrative have become touchpoints in contemporary arguments about gender equity and leadership within religious communities. Modern interpreters re-examine passages like these, using the silence around Adah, Zillah and Naamah, to critique traditions that continue to deny women authority or recognition. Their names become shorthand for a voiceless multitude: the mothers, wives, daughters, sisters, and female leaders whose stories have been assimilated into male-centered accounts of faith. As such, the way that communities read and remember Adah, Zillah and Naamah, becomes a litmus test for ongoing questions about; who is included in spiritual memory and who remains on the edge.

Silence as Theological Catalyst

Some interpretive models carve out space for meaningful engagement, not by filling in the blanks with imagined detail, but by embracing the tension of narrative absence. Theological inquiry grows not just from the content of scripture but also from its omissions. Adah, Zillah, and even <u>Naamah who is mentioned only one tine</u> in a short phase, inspire readers to ask why their voices disappear, pushing the faithful to reflect on spiritual authority that arises from the margins instead of the center. The process of questioning, remembering, and even lamenting the missing stories becomes an exercise in justice and creativity.

Rabbinic and academic perspectives often encourage active participation with difficult texts, turning silence into an invitation for communal memory work. This approach recognizes that absence need not spell defeat; it can serve as a foundation on which communities build a more inclusive and compassionate spiritual identity.

In this ongoing conversation, the nearly forgotten names of Adah, Zillah, and Naamah, continue to disrupt easy readings, drawing attention to the profound impact of those whom history neglects. Their presence challenges all who encounter sacred texts to honor the silenced and to treat omission itself as a starting point for faith, equity, and reimagined community

Summary and Reflections of this Topic

Now that we have explored the unique naming of **Adah and Zillah** as the <u>two wives</u> of Lamech, and **Naamah** as the <u>sister of</u> Tubal-cain, amid the silence surrounding most women in early Genesis (before the flood), we can see how their brief presence invites us to question who is remembered and why. Their mention challenges traditional male-centered narratives, urging readers to recognize the hidden stories and voices that shape scripture's message. By reflecting on these named yet largely silent figures, we open the door to deeper conversations about memory, authority, and gender within faith communities. This awareness encourages us to approach sacred texts with both humility and creativity—acknowledging **what is left unsaid** as much as what is recorded—and inspires ongoing efforts to recover and honor the forgotten women whose legacies continue to influence our understanding of history, spirituality, and justice today.

Part 3:

Time of Realization

Realization: U-Turn & Turning Point

José E. Espinoza

Chapter 14:

Rare & 'Sudden <u>Reattempt</u>'

How? Why? When?

(GENESIS 4:26)

"…*At that time people <u>began to call upon</u> the name of the Lord.*"

…<u>Invoking</u> God & <u>Reconnecting</u>

Humanity's Way <u>Back to God</u>: <u>Reconnection</u>, Restoration and More

From the earliest pages of the Bible; Starting on **Genesis 4:26,** a profound shift reshaped humanity's relationship with the divine. After the loss of Eden, direct and open communion with God gave way to distance, and new forms of connection marked by **"invocation"**, (perhaps in acts prayers, worships and rituals). This transition was not merely a change in religious practice, but a response to a deep, enduring human need to bridge a growing separation, from the Creator to the created human being. The stories of early <u>Reconnection</u> in Adoration, Invocation and worship, reveal that authentic devotion—rooted in the heart's intention rather than mere ceremony—became central to restoring what was broken. Across generations, these evolving acts of **'*calling upon God's name'** (*Invoking The Name of The Lord) according to **Genesis 4:26** reflect both; the challenges and hopes of a people striving, to remain connected to the holy amidst sin and alienation. This chapter offers a detailed look at how early humanity sought to reclaim intimacy with God through sacrifice, prayer, and ritual—a journey that laid the foundation for much of biblical worship and spiritual life thereafter.

Possibility of Interpretation 1:

Early Adoration and Worship Practices; After the Fall & <u>Before the Flood</u>

Vivid traces of <u>humanity's earliest longing for God,</u> emerge in the aftermath of Eden. When Adam and Eve were cast from paradise, the immediate sense of absence of the Celestial Father defined their lives. Cut off from direct communion, **their children instinctively reached upward**, <u>searching for ways to reconnect with their Creator and Divine Father</u>. The biblical account unfolds this spiritual striving through concrete acts of "Invoking <u>the Name of</u> The Lord." Within the 'Possibilities' of—offerings, sacrifices and worship—as fundamental expressions of hope and reverence.

Cain and Abel represent the first recorded worshipers (according to **Genesis 4:3-4**.), each bringing a gift to God from the fruits of their labor. Abel, a keeper of sheep, selected the firstborn of his flock, choosing the best and most valued. Cain, who tilled the ground, offered produce, but the text implies his gift lacked the same measure of sacrifice or devotion. God regarded Abel's offering with favor, while rejecting Cain's, highlighting that what mattered was not the outward act alone but the heart behind it. Abel's intention, his willingness to give what was precious, marked his sacrifice as genuine. Cain's, perhaps given without true faith or with indifference, set a sobering example of worship failing to please. These moments reveal early worship as more than duty—it became a language of desire, expressing both a plea for restored closeness and the willingness to honor God above self.

Each act of sacrifice simultaneously acknowledged loss and sought recompense. The first family, having lost paradise, brought forward what they had in a possible attempt to bridge the divide through adoration and petition. The offerings, simple though they may have been, signaled that even after estrangement, the desire for connection persisted. Sacrifice offered a way to speak to God in the absence of daily walking with Him. Petition and thanksgiving intertwined: these gifts asked for favor, yet also gave thanks, creating a basic but powerful framework for worship. The earliest sacrifices did not depend on elaborate ritual or complex rules. Sincerity, gratitude, and an understanding of relationship drove them, setting a precedent upheld throughout the unfolding biblical narrative.

As the generations advanced, (it is *possible that) *<u>worship gradually became more communal</u> and formalized. The birth of **Seth**, and later **Enosh**, signaled renewed hope that divine fellowship could be restored. In these times, calling upon the name of the Lord marked a shift from isolated attempts to a pattern of shared worship. The text in **Genesis 4:26** notes, ***"At that time people began to call upon the name of the Lord."*** Naming carried deep meaning among early peoples; names described hopes, character, or destiny. ***Enosh**'s own name, tied to *frailty and ***mortality***, reminded his generation of their need and dependence. It may have inspired greater humility and corporate worship—human finitude driving a collective reaching toward the infinite.

To **"call upon the name of the Lord"** possibly meant ***<u>returning to God in prayer, praise, and sacrifices</u>***. These acts, often performed around simple altars, created rituals that gathered families and later communities. Worship became less sporadic and more regular, woven into the rhythm of life. Sacrifices and prayers voiced not only individual longing, but also united people in the recognition of divine sovereignty and the hope for redemption. This transition from spontaneous offering to ritualized worship did not diminish the need for sincerity. <u>The lesson of Cain and Abel</u> lingered: <u>God continued to look beyond ceremony</u> for the **inner attitude of the heart**.

Concrete gatherings at altars and the invocation of God's name gave rise to traditions—rites that encouraged memory, gratitude, and belonging. Worship carried more than individual desire; it offered a sense of identity, binding groups through shared acts of reverence and reminding them of their place in a larger story of promise, fall, and hope. Early humans, aware of their brokenness, shaped their spiritual reconnection with The Creator, not for their own sake but as an answer to separation and longing for reconnection.

Throughout these nascent efforts, authenticity stood as the mark of true worship. Offerings given from the heart, sacrifices expressive of genuine dependence, and prayers formed in hope—as these became hallmarks, the distance between holy and human seemed a little less daunting. The journey was never simple, nor was resolution immediate. Yet within the steady rhythm of prayer, offering, and worshiping, a deep and persistent hope; flourished for restoration and reconciliation. The earliest generations, though distant from Eden, forged a path forward—one built on devotion, striving for honor, and a continual return to the God who had once walked among them.

Possibility of Interpretation 2:

Struggles and Joys in Maintaining Divine Connection

From the opening moments after the expulsion from Eden, humanity's experience of God shifted in profound ways. **Genesis 4:26** quietly signals a <u>moment of transformation</u>: ***"At that time people began to call on the name of the Lord."*** This phrase implies a new distance and a deep longing, for unlike Adam and Eve's open conversations with their Creator, <u>later generations could not approach God so freely</u>. Their interactions came to center around acts of calling, seeking, and worship—a transition visible in the stories of the earliest descendants, who lived in the echo of paradise lost and sought once again to hear the Almighty's voice.

Humanity faced the persistent reality of sin as a chasm cutting through every attempt at reconnection. The barrier went well beyond Adam and Eve's initial act of disobedience. In Cain's story, the sting of separation became even more pronounced. After the murder of Abel, God confronted Cain with his guilt, banishing him to wander the earth under the weight of a curse. No longer was there unbroken communion; instead, fear and alienation defined the human stance toward the divine (**Gen. 4:11-16**). This severed relationship led (possibly) to new rituals, sacrifices, and acts of devotion. The simple offerings of Abel and Cain demonstrated an early effort to reach across the divide, serving as prototypes for future acts of worship in which humanity, blocked from walking openly with God, could still attempt to draw near.

Desire for restoration did not fade but sparked new expressions of hope. Even as people struggled under the consequences of separation, their longing to reconnect (possibly) produced the turning point of prayers, offerings, and stories that pointed beyond their present condition. Prophetic dreams, (perhaps) with a possible vision of a future, where reconciliation might be complete. The hope that God would again act decisively, redeem, and restore His people filled the collective imagination. Devotion, in its many forms, became a sign of persistence—a statement that, although separated, humanity would not stop seeking the God from whom true life flows.

Amidst all these developments, the dynamics of worship and spiritual yearning defined what it meant to live after Eden. Possibly after this point: Rituals evolved into deep traditions. Hope survived each failure and setback. Faith was not mere belief but a lived pursuit, shaped by struggle, animated by glimpses of grace, and always oriented toward the promise of restoration, which would later find its greatest fulfillment in God's ongoing plan for humanity.

Summary & Reflections about this Topic

Understanding the early **efforts to <u>reconnect with God after the Fall & before the Flood</u>**, reveals a foundational story of human longing, worship, and hope that shapes the rest of biblical history. As readers and scholars, we can see **the possibility of** how sincere devotion moved from simple offerings to organized rituals, highlighting both the challenges and <u>possibilities of maintaining divine connection</u> amidst sin and separation. Now that we recognize this progression—from direct communion to mediated worship and the persistent desire for restoration—we can better appreciate the depth of humanity's spiritual journey and the enduring significance of God's covenantal grace. This insight invites us to explore how these early patterns continue to influence faith practices today, encouraging a heartfelt pursuit of God that balances tradition with authentic relationship.

Chapter 15:

Strange '<u>Return</u> to Kingdom # 1'

How? & <u>What Kingdom</u>?

(GENESIS 4:26)

…*"At that time <u>people began</u> to '<u>call on</u>' <u>The Name of The Lord</u>"*

The <u>Turning Point</u> and Humanity's Awakening; to Reestablish <u>The Kingdom of God</u> on Earth

More than six thousand years ago, after **God** the <u>**Creator** and</u> <u>**Supreme King**</u>; **ESTABLISHED** the **first human colony of <u>His</u>** <u>**Kingdom on earth**</u>, Placing <u>Adam and Eve</u> as Prime Ministers, Stewards, and Supervisors <u>in charge</u>; **The <u>Government of Heaven on</u>** <u>**earth**</u> **was Inaugurated.** Yet, due to the evident failure of the task from our forefathers according to Genesis 3:1-24, a **disconnection between humanity and the Divine Father and King happened.** Resulting as primary consequence; a Catastrophic **interruption** of the **plan and progress** of this Kingdom. Since Then, humanity faced a crisis deeper than any political upheaval or social collapse: a profound spiritual emptiness that fractured relationships and eroded harmony, justice, true purpose, peace, and much more.

Throughout generations, efforts to build cities, create culture, and seek power, failed <u>to fill the growing void within</u>. Yet amid this desolation, we can see here in **Genesis 4:26** as the first human's effort to reattempt the idea of The <u>Kingdom of God</u>. A quiet but revolutionary moment, that occurred *when <u>people</u> (for the first time mentioned in the Bible), <u>"called on the name of the Lord"</u>*. This act was not mere tradition or empty ritual.—It marked a radical turning point, signaling a collective **<u>awakening to something greater than human striving alone</u>**. Understanding this moment invites us to reflect on where we turn for <u>security</u> and <u>meaning</u> today, and how **<u>reconnecting with God as Sovereign King and loving Father</u>** can restore brokenness both ancient and present.

The <u>Cry for Restoration</u>: Humanity's Spiritual Awakening in Genesis 4:26

According to this biblical passage, a sense of emptiness shadowed humanity's early story, up to this point (before the flood). Genesis opens with the drama of creation and promise, but quickly, a somber pattern of spiritual separation emerges. Choices spiraled outwards from Adam and Eve's disobedience, leading to Cain's envy, Abel's murder, and the escalation of violence and self-exaltation through Cain's descendants. Generation after generation, people drifted further from their Creator. Relational fractures surfaced: brother turning against brother, families nursing wounds, violence increasingly worn like a badge of ingenuity. The chapters portray both the incredible ingenuity of human progress—cities built, arts created—and the cost of progress unmoored from the Creator's wisdom. Lamech, a descendant of Cain, sang of his own violent accomplishments, boasting of vengeance without remorse. As each generation inherited only a faint memory of God.

This backdrop of estrangement explains the profound weight behind Genesis 4:26, which describes a scattered, broken humanity reaching a point of spiritual exhaustion. The text says that ***<u>at that time</u> people began to call on the name of the Lord.***" In a world marked by spiritual desolation and generational neglect, this moment stands out as a turning point, a collective realization that to persist in isolation from God meant only more struggle and emptiness. Here, the movement is no longer simply the passive adoption of faith through ancestry. **<u>For the first time</u>**, individuals actively reached beyond despair for **reconnection**, no longer content to carry forward a distant tradition, but choosing instead <u>to ask for divine **restoration**</u>.

This shift came with urgency. Spiritual devastation was not abstract; it was seen in broken families, in prideful boasts about violence, in the normalization of evil as something worth celebrating. Earlier stories in Genesis show how alienation from God led to chaos: intimacy turned to suspicion, trust replaced by fear, and daily life framed by the instinct to protect, to avenge, and to survive alone. In this context, calling on the name of the Lord was not a casual prayer or ritual. It was a conscious act of surrender, a declaration of helplessness in the face of a world ruled by self-interest.

To "call on the name of the Lord" (to invoke) involves more than speaking God's title. It means turning toward God in hope, longing for a relationship restored, and openly admitting one's dependence on His sovereignty. This action is fueled by the recognition that nothing built—no city, no culture, no achievement—can heal the deep wounds that result from a life disconnected from God. To call upon His name signifies a willingness to be guided, corrected, and restored by the Creator's wisdom instead of one's own. It is the difference between inheriting a tradition and choosing faith anew, between living by inherited neglect and actively seeking the source of life.

This communal yearning marked the beginning of a new spiritual pursuit. Instead of breaking apart under the weight of alienation, a group of people collectively decided to turn to God, modeling a longing for life governed by something higher than human impulse or ambition. Their act was not weakness; it was the first step toward the rebuilding of trust, restoration of order, and the healing of spiritual wounds. History and present experience both show that attempts to govern life independently from God often produce chaos, competition, and cycles of disappointment. Consider a family fractured by secrets or a society built on the myth of 'self-sufficiency'. Such communities may achieve much but hope and belonging remain elusive.

Genesis 4:26 records not just a momentary revival but the birth of intentional spiritual restoration. This was a community awakening to its deep hunger for meaning, order, and reconciliation with the divine. By calling on God's name, they reached beyond cycles of brokenness, seeking hope that their lives, and those of their children, could be shaped by mercy and purpose rather than by repetition of past wounds.

<u>**This urge**—this longing for renewed relationship—**is as relevant now as it was then**</u>. When people sense the void created by spiritual neglect, the response modeled in Genesis 4:26 offers a pathway: admit the futility of going it alone, turn toward God, and allow a new legacy to begin. That longing stands as the foundation for transformation, beckoning all who are weary of life without divine order to seek God's leadership and restoration.

Restoring the Kingdom: Embracing <u>God as</u> <u>Sovereign King and</u> <u>Father</u>

Many adults today look for security and meaning in places that promise control but fail to deliver wholeness. Like the ancient world facing ruin and loneliness in Genesis, modern people often rally behind 'false kings'—their own ambition, the pursuit of status, devotion to productivity, or trust in cultural approval. These efforts to control life by personal merit imitate the <u>spiritual drift</u> described in Genesis, leading to exhaustion and broken connection with God. Take for example someone who throws everything into work achievements, hoping career success will guarantee satisfaction. The reward is fleeting, leaving a hollow longing for something more. The need to appear indispensable becomes a barrier to honest relationships and quiets the voice that aches for meaning beyond the next goal. These counterfeit sovereignties mimic autonomy but do not restore; they fragment the soul and crowd out God's reign.

Restoration does not end at obedience to a sovereign; <u>it awakens identity</u>. Genesis 4:26 is not only about seeking God's kingship but also **<u>remembering who we are</u>**—<u>God's beloved children</u>. Adults, shaped by performance culture, often lose sight of this. When worldly success or approval falters, emptiness threatens. A believer who failed in business described finding comfort in God's acceptance. Sitting with Scripture, he reminded himself, "God calls me His own." Self-worth rooted in God's love stayed strong even when visible marks of success disappeared.

José E. Espinoza

Embracing God as Father

Use these steps to affirm your true identity:

- Write down what you believe gives you value (talents, looks, social standing).
- Compare your list with biblical truths: "You are God's child, chosen and dearly loved."
- Cross out false sources of worth. Replace with statements like, "I belong to God. He delights in me."
- Repeat these truths daily, especially when facing discouragement or rejection.
- Thank God for claiming you as His own.

Genesis 4:26's model was not a one-time act. Calling on God was continual—a daily habit fostering real relationship. Restoration under God's kingship demands consistent action, not passive hope. **Prayer and walking in God's ways cultivate lasting change.**

Active Pursuit

Try this daily spiritual practice:

- Start each morning by inviting God's reign: "Father, I invite You to lead my day."
- Read a short Scripture passage. Ask what it reveals about God's rule.
- In every choice—small or big—pause and ask, "Does this honor God as King?"
- Review your day at night. Notice where peace replaced anxiety or obedience grew.
- Record changes in perspective or relationships over time, giving thanks for God's faithfulness.

In practical ways, these habits heal fragmentation and bring step-by-step renewal, echoing the call first made in Genesis 1:26, to turn from desolation and trust the living God. This continual reaching to God for guidance and identity reignites spiritual life and restores belonging as part of God's restored family

Summary & Reflections about this Chapter

Now that we understand the profound significance of Genesis 4:26 as humanity's first intentional turn to God, we can embrace a renewed commitment to calling on the Lord daily, recognizing Him as our Sovereign King and loving Father. This chapter invites us to move beyond inherited faith or empty striving and instead cultivate a living relationship grounded in surrender, trust, and identity in God. By identifying and releasing counterfeit sovereignties that fragment our souls, and by practicing regular submission to God's guidance, we open ourselves to true restoration and peace. As we apply these biblical truths thoughtfully and intentionally, we participate in the ongoing work of healing brokenness and building communities shaped by divine wisdom and mercy. The call to "call on the name of the Lord" remains as urgent and transformative now as it was then—offering each of us a path from spiritual emptiness to abundant life under God's faithful reign.

CONCLUSION

At this point, when our journey through these early chapters of 'Strange Topics' in Genesis (1:1 – 4:26), draws to a close, we find ourselves standing at the edge of mystery—a place where ancient questions echo into our own time. These stories are more than distant legends or tales for children; they pulse with living questions about who we are, why we long for connection, and how we respond to the challenges that shadow every life. What began in the stillness of Eden—out of dust, breath, and divine intention—unfolded into a drama marked by innocence, wonder, choice, loss, and the persistent desire for restoration. And at each step, we have encountered symbols and enigmas that defy easy explanation: strange days without sun, a plural-speaking God, a serpent that debates, fruit whose identity remains veiled, garments of skin that both cover and reveal, a sword guarding the path home, and the mysterious mark upon an outcast brother.

Reflecting on all we have explored, a common thread emerges—a deep tension between clarity and ambiguity, between what is revealed and what remains shrouded. The creation story opens not with simple answers, but with layers of meaning that invite humility and curiosity. **Is "day one" a span of 24 hours**, an age beyond counting, or the poetry of God's purposes unfolding outside our clocks? This lack of certainty is no defect; instead, it makes the text living and dynamic, urging us to grapple with the nature of time, the rhythm of existence, and the limitations of human understanding. Like the first readers, we stand before these mysteries called not to mastery, but to reverent questioning, learning to measure our lives not only by hours, but by moments of presence, purpose, and wonder.

The story's heart beats strongest when we encounter the possibility that God's nature is itself a paradox—one and yet expressed in deliberate plural, hinting at layers of community and relationship even within divinity. **The phrase *"Let us make man in our image"*** stretches us beyond narrow definitions, asking us to think again about unity, difference, collaboration, and love. Whether we interpret these words as a conversation among heavenly beings or a glimpse of the triune Godhead foreshadowed in Christian faith, the effect is the same: our place in this world is marked by dignity and calling. Each person reflects, however imperfectly, the richness and depth of the divine image, tasked not only with survival, but with representing care, creativity, and moral responsibility.

Yet, Genesis never lets us live long in idealized innocence. The moment when **humanity wakes to its own nakedness** is a turning point not only for Adam and Eve, but for all who follow—<u>an awakening that brings shame</u>, self-consciousness, and the enduring struggle between openness and concealment. That their first instinct was to **cover themselves with fig leaves** speaks to the way we grasp at whatever comes to hand to hide our wounds and failures. But the story does not end with human improvisation; **God's act of clothing them in animal skins** signals His enduring concern, revealing a grace that meets us even in exile and vulnerability. Here, the earliest garment becomes the beginning of a much longer conversation about mercy: a gift offered not because we deserve it, but because God will not leave us alone or exposed.

In **the serpentine figure lurking in Eden's garden**, we confront the presence of evil—not as brute force, but <u>as cunning, rational,</u> and ambiguous. Whether seen as a literal tempter, a vessel of satanic intent, or a symbol of desire and doubt, the serpent introduces intellectual complexity, abuse of free will, and negligence of moral risk. Its questions are timeless: Did God really say? Can you not decide for yourself? The fruit becomes the tangible sign of longing for knowledge, autonomy, and experience—gifts that bring both awakening and sorrow. **Whatever the "fruit" truly was,** its elusiveness has kept generations pondering the boundaries of wisdom, innocence, rebellion, and grace. <u>The consequence of eating is immediate</u>, yet also endlessly unfolding; our search for knowledge never ends, but always carries costs.

One of the most powerful lessons rises from the aftermath: boundaries appear where once there was open access, and exile becomes the shared experience of humanity. **Flaming swords bar the gate**, cherubim keep watch, and the tree of life stands behind impassable thresholds. Yet, even here, the restriction is not only punishment—it is protection and hope. <u>By closing the way to eternal life in a fallen state</u>, God preserves the possibility for healing, redemption, and ultimate reunion. Mortality, once feared, is transformed into a space where change can happen, where grace can interrupt cycles of violence, vengeance, and despair.

As humanity spreads across the earth, the marks of Cain and the silence around so many women in early genealogies tell further stories about the complexity of judgment, mercy, and memory. The mark or **sign placed on Cain** is neither condemnation nor unqualified defense; it confronts us with the reality that justice and compassion are rarely simple, that consequences coexist with preservation. The brief mention of **Adah, Zillah, and Naamah alone** among pre-flood women, shines light on the silences that fill sacred history—reminding us that scripture's gaps are also invitations to remember those whom tradition forgets, to seek out lost voices, and to <u>challenge old exclusions</u> with new vision.

Against the growing tide of alienation, violence, and fractured community, Genesis offers a note of hope—quiet, almost overlooked, yet profound. **When people begin to "call on the name of the Lord,"** a turning point is reached. The endless cycle of striving, building, failing, and wounding is interrupted by a deliberate act of invocation, surrender, and trust. This moment signals more than nostalgia for lost paradise; it is the seed of spiritual renewal, the first movement toward restoration and reconciliation. Here, spirituality or **Godliness is not mere ritual, but a return to relationship**—a willingness to **let God be King and Father once again**, to root identity in divine love rather than in personal achievement or social approval.

If there is any final lesson to draw from these foundational stories, it is this: the journey to understand our origins is inseparable from the journey back to God. We do not passively inherit faith or wholeness; we must choose it over and over, in small actions and great risks, in daily prayers and lifelong commitments. This book (and primarily the bible) calls us to lay down the false kings—the illusions of control, the pride of independence—and to let our truest worth be shaped by God's gracious acceptance and continual guidance. As we call on His name, even amid bewilderment and brokenness, He responds with presence, mercy, and a promise that the story—our story—is not finished.

José E. Espinoza

So, as readers, scholars, seekers, and believers, let us continue the work begun in Eden: to face mystery with humility, to pursue knowledge with caution and courage, to honor each other as God's image-bearer with dignity, and above all, to keep our hearts open to the God who speaks from both cloud and silence. In doing so, we answer the ancient invitation to participate in the ongoing restoration of creation, and to walk—however falteringly—toward the fullness of life purpose intended from the very beginning.

STRANGE TOPICS *Book #1*

Reference List of Each Chapter

Reference List of Chapter 1:

Creation's Praise of God: An Ecological Theology of Non-Human and Human Being - ProQuest. (2025). Proquest.com. https://search.proquest.com/openview/5d8e6ff1c1baaccd4b01e932fa419654/1?pq-origsite=gscholar&cbl=51922&diss=y

House, C. P. (2024, December 2). *How Should Christians Understand the "Days" of Creation in Genesis? - Christian Publishing House Blog*. Christian Publishing House Blog. https://christianpublishinghouse.co/2024/12/02/how-should-christians-understand-the-days-of-creation-in-genesis/

Niessen, R. (1980, March 1). *Theistic Evolution and the Day-Age Theory*. Www.icr.org. https://www.icr.org/article/theistic-evolution-day-age-theory

Reference List of Chapter 2:

Darville, J. (2023, June 9). *The Trinity in Genesis 1 (and Why it Matters)*. Christ and Culture. https://cfc.sebts.edu/faith-and-culture/the-trinity-in-genesis-1-and-why-it-matters/

Farris, J. (2022). *Substance Dualist Theological Anthropology*. St Andrews Encyclopaedia of Theology. https://www.saet.ac.uk/Christianity/SubstanceDualistTheologicalAnthropology

Interpretive Challenges in the OT #1: Genesis 1:26. (2009, April 13). Josh Philpot. https://joshphilpot.com/2009/04/13/interpretive-problems-in-the-ot-1-genesis-126/

Peterson, R. S. (2016, January 21). *The Imago Dei as Human Identity*. Penn State Press.

Reference List of Chapter 3:

Andrews, E. D. (2024, October 8). *Death, the Soul, and Immortality*. Christian Pub House. https://www.christianpublishers.org/post/death-the-soul-and-immortality

Youvan, D. C. (2025, March 11). *The Dual Nature of Humanity: Interpreting Genesis 1:27 and 2:7 Across Theological, Philosophical, and Sociopolitical Paradigms*. https://doi.org/10.13140/RG.2.2.30107.78884

Youvan, D. C. (2024, June 2). *Two Types of Man in Genesis: A Philosophical and Esoteric Interpretation*. https://doi.org/10.13140/RG.2.2.21361.08807

www.wisdomlib.org. (2025, June 17). *The Concept of the Immortality of the Soul: A Biblical-Theological Study*. Wisdomlib.org. https://www.wisdomlib.org/christianity/journal/e-journal-of-religious-and-theological-studies/d/doc1668869.html

Reference List of Chapter 4:

Garb. (2015). *Shame as an Existential Emotion in Modern Kabbalah*. Jewish Social Studies. https://doi.org/10.2979/jewisocistud.21.1.03

Westerlund, F. (2023, July 21). *Exposed: On Shame and Nakedness*. Philosophia; Springer Science+Business Media. https://doi.org/10.1007/s11406-023-00668-3

Reference List of Chapter 5:

José E. Espinoza

Adjei, E. G. (2024, October 21). *A Historical - Grammatical Study of Genesis 3:15, the Seedbed of the Theme of Enmity in Genesis*. International Journal of Religion. https://doi.org/10.61707/xgrdzs03

Burda, G. (2025). *THIRD Chapter Commentaries on the Bible*. Scribd. https://www.scribd.com/document/196474795/THIRD-Chapter-Commentaries-on-the-Bible

Genesis 3 Commentary | Precept Austin. (n.d.). Www.preceptaustin.org. https://www.preceptaustin.org/genesis-3-commentary

Hundley, M. (2022). *Non-Priestly Genesis and Exodus*. Cambridge Core; Cambridge University Press. https://www.cambridge.org/core/books/yahweh-among-the-gods/nonpriestly-genesis-and-exodus/47F91EF32B3D124512D7940928421568

Reference List of Chapter 6:

Animal Suffering in an Unfallen World: a Theodicy of Non-Human Evolution - ProQuest. (2015). Proquest.com. https://search.proquest.com/openview/d7b499cf79253e3926d13c2a4ce7e94d/1?pq-origsite=gscholar&cbl=51922&diss=y

Dolansky, S. (2022, January 4). *How the Serpent in the Garden Became Satan*. Biblical Archaeology Society. https://www.biblicalarchaeology.org/daily/biblical-topics/bible-interpretation/how-the-serpent-in-the-garden-became-satan/

Genesis 3 Commentary | Precept Austin. (n.d.). Www.preceptaustin.org. https://www.preceptaustin.org/genesis-3-commentary

View. (2014, April 8). *Death Before the Fall*. Alastair's Adversaria. https://alastairadversaria.com/2014/04/08/death-before-the-fall/

Reference List of Chapter 7:

Anna-Maria Moubayed. (2023, April 29). *The Charisma of Fruits: From Greek Mythology to Genesis*. Religions; Multidisciplinary Digital Publishing Institute. https://doi.org/10.3390/rel14050585

Brennan, A., & Lo, Y.-S. (2021, December 3). *Environmental Ethics*. Stanford Encyclopedia of Philosophy. https://plato.stanford.edu/entries/ethics-environmental/

Genesis 3 Commentary | Precept Austin. (n.d.). Www.preceptaustin.org. https://www.preceptaustin.org/genesis-3-commentary

Sijuwade, J. (2025, June 20). *King Jesus of Nazareth: An Evidential Inquiry*. Religions; Multidisciplinary Digital Publishing Institute. https://doi.org/10.3390/rel16070808

Reference List of Chapter 8:

Cornwall, R. (2017, November 15). *Disciples of Christ and the Problem of Sin – Part One*. Bobcornwall.com; Blogger. https://www.bobcornwall.com/2017/11/disciples-of-christ-and-problem-of-sin.html

One For Israel. (2016, June 2). *The Symbolism of Figs in the Bible*. ONE for ISRAEL Ministry. https://www.oneforisrael.org/bible-based-teaching-from-israel/figs-in-the-bible/

The Editors of Encyclopaedia Britannica. (2019). *Original sin | theology | Britannica*. Encyclopædia Britannica. https://www.britannica.com/topic/original-sin

Vise, D. L. (2025, April 15). *The Remnant Newspaper - The Tree of Knowledge of Good and Evil: The Fall, the Fig Tree, and the Restoration of the Garments of Light*. The Remnant Newspaper. https://www.remnantnewspaper.com/web/index.php/fetzen-fliegen/item/7701-the-tree-of-knowledge-of-good-and-evil-the-fall-the-fig-tree-and-the-restoration-of-the-garments-of-light

Reference List of Chapter 9:

Gane, R. E. (2023, June 16). *Sacrifice and the Old Testament*. St Andrews Encyclopaedia of Theology. https://www.saet.ac.uk/Christianity/SacrificeandtheOldTestament

Genesis 3:21 Commentaries: The LORD God made garments of skin for Adam and his wife, and clothed them. (2019). Biblehub.com. https://biblehub.com/commentaries/genesis/3-21.htm

Marx, B. (2021). *Clothing and Exchange of Garments in the Bible, as a Picture of God's Dealings with His People*. Evangelical Review of Theology. https://www.academia.edu/44987339/Clothing_and_Exchange_of_Garments_in_the_Bible_as_a_Picture_of_God_s_Dealings_with_His_People

Myers, J. (2014, July 2). *Did God Perform the First Sacrifice in Genesis 3:21?* Redeeming God. https://redeeminggod.com/first-sacrifice-genesis-3_21/

Reference List of Chapter 10:

Genesis 3:24 | Bible Study Tools | TrulyRandomVerse.com. (2015). Trulyrandomverse.com. https://trulyrandomverse.com/genesis/3-24

Genesis 3 Bible Commentary and Meaning - Video Bible. (2024, October 15). Video Bible. https://www.videobible.com/bible-commentary/genesis-3

The Guardians of Eden, the Mysterious Cherubim & Their Symbolism - Redemptive Bible Studies. (2022, August 7). Redemptive Bible Studies - Where Ethics and Eschatology Meet. https://redemptivebiblestudies.com/the-mysterious-cherubim-their-symbolism/

What Is a Cherub? The Cherubim in the Bible. (n.d.). Christianity.com. https://www.christianity.com/wiki/angels-and-demons/what-is-a-cherub-the-cherubim-in-the-bible.html

Reference List of Chapter 11:

Jabr, F. (2023). *John A. Long - Publications List*. Publicationslist.org.

Jenks. (2018). *A Tale of Two Trees: Delinking Death from Sin by Viewing Genesis 2–3 Independently from Paul*. Bulletin for Biblical Research. https://doi.org/10.5325/bullbiblrese.28.4.0533

Sifeddine Soltane. (2024, June 12). *Exploring Esotericism, Myth, the Collective Unconscious, and its Symbolism in Carl Jung's The Red Book*. ResearchGate; unknown. https://doi.org/10.13140/RG.2.2.12122.96968

Yadav, R. (2024). *The Theology of the Book of Genesis*. Academia.edu. https://www.academia.edu/125751860/The_Theology_of_the_Book_of_Genesis

Reference List of Chapter 12:

Duncan, D. L. (1998, August 9). *The Beginnings of Culture*. Reformed Theological Seminary. https://rts.edu/resources/the-beginnings-of-culture/

Jones, C. P. (2023). *Understanding the Lamanite Mark*. Interpreter: A Journal of Latter-Day Saint Faith and Scholarship. https://journal.interpreterfoundation.org/understanding-the-lamanite-mark/

Enigmatic Biblical Phenomena: In Genesis 1 - 4

José E. Espinoza

Matthew 1. (2024). Netbible.org. http://netbible.org/#

Sauter, M. (2019, April 12). *What Happened to Cain in the Bible?* Biblical Archaeology Society. https://www.biblicalarchaeology.org/daily/biblical-topics/bible-interpretation/what-happened-to-cain-in-the-bible/

Reference List of Chapter 13:

Genesis 1-11 NET - - Bible Gateway. (n.d.). Www.biblegateway.com. https://www.biblegateway.com/passage/?search=Genesis%201-11&version=NET

Lynch, M. J. (2025, July 7). *The Roots of Violence: Male Violence against Women in Genesis | The Biblical Mind*. Center for Hebraic Thought. https://thebiblicalmind.org/article/male-violence-against-women-in-genesis/

Matthew 1. (2024). Netbible.org. http://netbible.org/#

Woolstenhulme, K. J. (2020, December 24). *The Matriarchs in Genesis Rabbah*. Bloomsbury Publishing.

Reference List of Chapter 14:

Baugher, C. (2025). *Genesis*. Knowingthebible.net. https://www.knowingthebible.net/bible-studies/genesis

Coulter, D. (2024, January 11). *Bible Study: Genesis 4 - Daniel Coulter - Medium*. Medium. https://medium.com/@coulter.daniel/bible-study-genesis-4-2a641ec90602

Card, B. (2018, November 16). *GENESIS REVEALED – LESSON 4 - Firestorm Ministries, International*. Firestorm Ministries, International. https://firestormministry.com/genesis-revealed-lesson-4/

Worshiping the Lord: Genesis 4:26. (2018, January 19). Redemptive History and Theology. https://redemptivehistorytheology.com/blog/chapter-3-calling-on-the-name-of-the-lord-genesis-425-26/worshiping-the-lord/

Reference List of Chapter 15:

Genesis 4:26 Meaning - Video Bible. (2024, August 14). Video Bible. https://www.videobible.com/meaning/genesis-4-26

Genesis 4:1-26 Daily Bible Devotions. (2025). LifePoint Church - MN. https://www.lifepointchurchmn.com/blog/2025/03/23/genesis-4-1-26-daily-bible-devotions

Prayer for Freedom from Habitual Sins. (2025). Wildatheart.org. https://wildatheart.org/prayer/prayer-freedom-habitual-sins/

Prayer of Consecration. (2025). Wildatheart.org. https://wildatheart.org/prayer/prayer-consecration/

About The Author

José E. Espinoza is a Writer, Instructor, and Christian guide specializing in **Leadership** and personal development for young adults, experienced individuals, and professionals. He has been a dedicated **Missionary** since his youth, consistently committed to sharing **the evangelical message of the Kingdom of God.**

José E. Espinoza

Other books from The Author

Available on Amazon:

Message of Jesus #1

Proclamation of the Kingdom of Heaven on Earth as Primary Objective

----------o----------

NEW LIFE
In 3 Priorities of
TRIUMPH
Transformation ABC
In The Kingdom of God

----------o----------

TIME, TALENT, TREASURE

Human Life equation

Awareness for a Meaningful Life Existence

----------o----------